Mergers & Acquisitions Made Simple

Step by Step M&A, Company Valuation, Negotiation Skills, Business Plans and Finance Guide for Startup Founders and Entrepreneurs

UMRAN NAYANI

© 2021 UMRAN NAYANI | **ONECALL** Business Solutions

Magically Simple Mobile Commerce

www.ecomgenieapp.com

●necall.ai
Business Solutions

© Copyright Umran Nayani. All Rights Reserved.
Copyright Protected with www.ProtectMyWork.com,
Reference Number: 15755270122S047

All intellectual property rights are reserved. This publication cannot be reproduced in any form or by any means, electronic or mechanical, including photocopying, recording, or any information browsing, storage, or retrieval system, without the express written permission of the publisher.

The publisher and author accept no responsibility for any errors, inaccuracies, omissions, or other inconsistencies in this publication, even though it is aimed to give accurate information on the subject matter discussed.

This publication is intended to provide readers with useful information, but it is not intended to substitute direct expert guidance. If this level of assistance is required, a qualified professional should be contacted.

All of the characters and events in this book are fictional unless otherwise stated.

Cover Design: Maria Azka

Table of Contents

SECTION 1 | INTRODUCTION TO MERGERS AND ACQUISITIONS MADE SIMPLE 8

Chapter 1: Welcome to Mergers and Acquisitions - A Framework to Selling Businesses 8

Chapter 2: My Personal View on Mergers and Acquisitions 10

Chapter 3: Overview of the Mergers and Acquisitions Process 21

SECTION 2 | WHAT DOES THE TERM MERGERS AND ACQUISITIONS MEAN? 30

Chapter 4: What does the Term Mergers and Acquisitions Mean - Overview? 30

Chapter 5: What Separates a Merger from an Acquisition? 32

Chapter 6: Why Do Businesses Merge? 35

Chapter 7: Why Do Organizations Make Acquisitions? 39

Chapter 8: What exactly do we mean by "Synergies"? 43

Chapter 9: What are the Role of Advisory in the Mergers and Acquisitions Market? 47

Chapter 10: Financing an Acquisition through Capital Raising 51

Chapter 11: How Are Companies Valued in the M&A Market? 54

Chapter 12: The Mergers and Acquisitions Market 57

Chapter 13: Deal Strategy for Mergers and Acquisitions 61

SECTION 3 | HOW TO VALUE A BUSINESS IN CORPORATE FINANCE: A CRASH COURSE? 65

Chapter 14: The Business Valuation Crash Course: An Introduction to Company Valuation 65

Chapter 15: Valuation of a Firm for Sale 68

Chapter 16: Balance Sheet and P&L Statement: The Financial Statements Are the Two Key Sets of Information You'll Need to Know 71

Chapter 17: Learn the Fundamentals of Corporate Finance in this Crash Course on Company Valuation & Cash flow Methods 75

Chapter 18: The Weighted Average Cost of Capital in Corporate Finance: Calculating the WACC - The Corporate Finance Crash Course 78

Chapter 19: The Weighted Average Cost of Capital Calculation in Corporate Finance - Corporate Finance Crash Course 81

Chapter 20: A More Detailed Look at the Terminal Value 83

Chapter 21: Corporate Finance Crash Course: Common Valuation Errors 85

SECTION 4 | PRE PLANNING 88

Chapter 22: How to Get the Most Value When You Sell Your Company 88

Chapter 23: Understanding the Sale Procedure 90

Chapter 24: When to Sell a Company - The Importance of Transaction Timeliness 96

Chapter 25: Planning for the Sale of a Business 99

Chapter 26: Selling a Business - Objectives During the Sale 103

Chapter 27: Selling a Business: Pre-sale preparedness introduction 107

Chapter 28: Selling a Business - Rules and Regulations (Legal and Admin Formalities) 110

Chapter 29: Selling a Business - Operational Preparedness Undertaking 113

Chapter 30: Selling a Business - Review of the Company Assets 116

SECTION 5 | THE PROCESS OF SELLING A BUSINESS 121

Chapter 31: Selling a Business - Memorandum for Information Preparation 121

Chapter 32: Selling a Business - Choosing the Best Buyers 124

Chapter 33: Selling a Business - Segmentation of Buyers 128

Chapter 34: Selling a Business – Brace yourself for Due Diligence 133

SECTION 6 | MARKETING THE COMPANY 136

Chapter 35: The Deal's Success Depends on This Key Element 136

Chapter 36: Selling a Business - In the deal process, ... 139

SECTION 7 | WHAT IS THE PROCEDURE FOR SELLING TO PRIVATE EQUITY INVESTORS? 143

Chapter 37: A Guide to Selling Your Firm Under a Buyout Deal 143

Chapter 38: The Sale Procedure 144

Chapter 39: What is an MBO - Management Buyout, and how does it work? 146

Chapter 40: How to Value a Business in an MBO 148

Chapter 41: How Do Private Equity Firm Value a Company? 150

Chapter 42: Increasing the Exit Value 152

Chapter 43: What is EBIT and EBITDA? 154

Chapter 44: Business Assets 156

Chapter 45: What does it mean when I say "Debt-Free" or "Cash-Free?" 157

Chapter 46: What is Normalized Working Capital, and how does it work? 158

Chapter 47: The Working Capital Cycle 159

Chapter 48: Mastering Normalized Working Capital Negotiation 160

Chapter 49: Buyout Summary 162

SECTION 8: TERM SHEETS FOR BEGINNERS: A GUIDE TO VENTURE CAPITAL INVESTING 163

Chapter 50: What is a Term Sheet - Part 1 163

Chapter 51: What is a Term Sheet - Part 2 168

Chapter 52: Term Sheets: Key Concepts 174

Chapter 53: What Are Term Sheets Trying to Accomplish? 179

SECTION 9 | LOI IN MERGERS AND ACQUISITIONS 184

Chapter 54: LOIs and MOUs Introduction 184

Chapter 55: MOUs and LOIs in Mergers and Acquisitions 186

Chapter 56: LOI's Binding or Non-Binding? 187

Chapter 57: The Benefits and Drawbacks of LOIs 188

Chapter 58: The Key Components of LOIs Part 1 190

Chapter 59: The Key Components of LOIs - Part 2 192

Chapter 60: A Sample of a UK Style LOI 196

Chapter 61: An Sample of a US-Style LOI 199

Chapter 62: Summary and Additional Resources 201

SECTION 10: THE DUE DILIGENCE PROCEDURE 203

Chapter 63: Due Diligence: What is It and Why Is it Important? 203

Chapter 64: Use Virtual Data Rooms to Your Advantage 205

Chapter 65: People Management - Processes 207

Chapter 66: Key Takeaways from Our Process of Doing Deep Due Diligence 208

Chapter 67: Virtual Data Room - Activity 210

SECTION 11 | WHAT IS NEGOTIATION AND HOW DOES IT WORK? 211

Chapter 68: What is Negotiation? 211

Chapter 69: Negotiation Fundamentals 212

Chapter 70: Value Exchange Principle 214

Chapter 71: Negotiation Objectives 216

SECTION 12: PROCESSES FOR NEGOTIATION AND TRANSACTION MANAGEMENT 218

Chapter 72: Negotiation Theory 218

Chapter 73: Negotiation Preparation 220

Chapter 74: Management of Transaction Processes 222

Chapter 75: Key Learning's from the World of Conducting Negotiations and Managing Transaction Processes 224

Chapter 76: Schedule of Events - Activity 228

SECTION 13: THE SALE AND PURCHASE AGREEMENT 230

Chapter 77: Sale and Purchase Agreement 230

Chapter 78: Concurrent Drafting 231

Chapter 79: What are the Most Important Topics to Address During Negotiation? 232

Chapter 80: Complexities and Issues That May Arise 235

Chapter 81: Market Analyzer - Deal Review and Deal Breakers Checklist 236

SECTION 14: GETTING YOUR BUSINESS READY FOR A MERGER OR ACQUISITION - CLOSING THE DEAL 238

Chapter 82: It's Not Only About the Money 239

Chapter 83: Actions are more powerful than words. 240

Chapter 84: Everything is Negotiable (Even When You've Signed) 241

SECTION 15: CLOSING THE DEAL 242

Chapter 85: Overcoming Obstacles While Closing an M&A Deal 242

Chapter 86: Keep the Principals Involved 244

Chapter 87: Closing Deal Points 245

Chapter 88: Deal Closing - Timing 246

Chapter 89: Closing - Complexities 247

Chapter 90: In Person or Virtual Closing? 248

Chapter 91: Activity: Deal Closing Checklist 249

SECTION 16: SUMMARY AND WRAP UP 251

Chapter 92 - Summary and Wrap Up 251

Chapter 93: Bonus Resources You Wouldn't Want to Miss 253

Section 1 | Introduction to Mergers and Acquisitions Made Simple

Chapter 1: Welcome to Mergers and Acquisitions - A Framework to Selling Businesses

Hello and welcome to Mergers & Acquisitions - a framework to selling businesses, with an emphasis on M&A, company valuation, negotiation skills, business plans, and finance.

My name is Umran Nayani. I've worked on closing agreements nationally and internationally for nearly a decade, with a wide variety of organizations of many different sizes and kinds. And I'm ecstatic to be able to share my expertise with you here.

Now, I'll tell you that this book will be my silo for all of my corporate finance knowledge. You won't have to go anyplace else if you're looking for this data in my book's portfolio; this is where you'll find it.

I'm excited to share my story with you. But, of course, it's a complicated topic, which means we'll have to go into depth on many issues in order to try to convey some of the key aspects of it.

So I'm going to start off with an introduction to the subject and the procedure, then go through a simple yet entertaining explanation of the whole M&A business, how it works, and what all the jargon means.

Then, for the sake of completeness, I'll give you a quick crash course on valuation.

Now, this may appear to be a lot at first, but I want you to understand how crucial it is to get valuations correct.

At the same time, however, it is quite tough. It's mostly as art.

Then we'll move on to a set of stages in the book where we'll walk you through the process of turning a firm into a viable business.

So we'll go through the first stage of planning, the presale preparation, and then we'll go over how to conduct a sale.

We then shift our attention to marketing the company and addressing some of the key concerns.

In this section, which is entitled "Fascinating Deal Analysis," we'll discuss the distinctions between deal and company sales. We'll also go over how to look at a sale in negotiation if you're doing a buyout, as well as some of the things that are particularly essential for financial investors and trade buyers.

I'll then go over some of the difficulties in term sheets. I'd also like to give you a quick heads up on negotiations.

This part, in particular, may develop further. I could write a book on negotiation. As a result, covering this subject in just four chapters is quite difficult. However, I'm hoping that you'll obtain an idea of how vital negotiation is as a skill.

Then we finish the book and depart on our own.

I'm ecstatic to tell you about it. I'm hoping you find it very exciting.

Now, keep in mind that I'm here to assist you if you need assistance or have any questions. If you have any ideas for additional things to include in the book, please contact me (umran@onecallbusinesssolutions.com). We can make the experience better by working together.

Please consider leaving your honest feedback as a rating and review for the book, as well as any other thoughts that come to mind.

If you have any comments or queries before leaving a rating interview, please contact me so that I may address them for you rather than leaving them unanswered since this approach you'll truly help everyone.

I'm not going to tell you what to say or how to evaluate it. That's entirely up to you. Of course, I'll take everything you have to say into account.

A warm welcome, a complicated subject. I'm hoping you'll find it challenging and enjoyable.

Chapter 2: My Personal View on Mergers and Acquisitions

I've been in business for almost ten years, and I'd want to offer you my personal viewpoint on acquisitions and mergers.

The major issue is how to teach something like mergers and acquisitions in a way that makes sense?

Because it's a complicated subject and a complex procedure. You wouldn't necessarily find a textbook blueprint for execution. The simple answer is that you can only really teach it by example.

So you want to know that the individual telling their story with you has actually been there, done it. I have a T-shirt for that.

It's great to have spent a few years working as a Spend Analyst, but it's even better when you've also spent some time in the trenches.

There is no way to acquire this expertise by simply reading about it. You do need to work on transactions and have that knowledge.

I am looking to draw from my experience and personal research. So, when I'm working on new contracts, trust that you'll get access to the insights.

I'd also want to share my views on what it's like to be involved in mergers and acquisitions.

The business cycle is, I believe, the starting point. If you believe that every industry has a life cycle, the market is full of these firms, all of which have their own lifecycle.

Essentially, it's all about generating value.

Entrepreneurs start businesses because they want to build something and make money.

The law of gravity is always at work. The businesses in this group are expected to develop. They need money to expand, and they may have to take over other companies.

Then, at the end of the day, entrepreneurs will want some type of exit, whether it's partial or whole.

They sell the firm to someone else. They can't realize value for themselves unless they do so.

So you have a mechanism in place where entrepreneurs are busy building businesses, but they require access to capital and ultimately need to be able to extract money. Then we have the next stage: mergers and acquisitions. That's when integrations and acquisitions really come in handy.

So, if you start with a company lifecycle, you've got a startup that invents a product and creates it and does all the research and development, then goes looking for a customer.

Now, if one customer purchases a product that isn't really genuine evidence, you may have 100s, 1000s of hundreds of thousands of clients who buy your goods and have a 'Product-Market' fit.

So the business is progressing. They now require access to funding in these early phases.

It's then necessary to put money in. It's practically impossible to start a business from scratch without any external investment.

The company needs to grow and scale when it has obtained a group of consumers.

Before you get any money at all, you need to buy supplies and pay staff, meaning your cash flow is diminished by the time the sale has finished. Working capital is required.

Now, at some point, it must consider how it will exit, how well it'll perform, and how the entrepreneurs, investors will be able to sell or IPO or buyout the firm. That manner may be via a sale or an IPO or a buyout.

They may have to complete an acquisition as a part of their development. The business may combine with another firm.

M&A are, by definition, all-encompassing.

Because you may have an acquisition, it includes a firm's sale. The other side of an acquisition, however, is not the sale side.

Mergers and acquisitions also include company exits.

IPOs are a specialized topic. You'll need extensive expertise of your market's listing rules in order to do that. And you must be able to go through all of the steps and documentation involved in doing so.

However, that is a distinct set of abilities, and it's typically handled by a stockbroker rather than an investment banker.

So, what are the most important things to remember as an advisor?

Basically, you'll need to offer the firm strategic counsel. You must become involved and understand what they're trying to accomplish in order to offer them advice.

From your experience in the sector, you know what they want to accomplish, so they will undoubtedly want to raise capital at some point. It's more likely to be through private or institutional investors, such as private equity or venture capital, in the early stages.

The firm may want or need to make acquisitions. As a result, you'll have to assist them on the buy-side in locating and obtaining bids from businesses before organizing everything and securing the funding for it.

Then, when it comes to sales, you must assist them in realizing their investment.

That might be achieved through a complete exit or by working with a stock broker to have an IPO.

Let's take a closer look at some of the market actors in the M&A environment.

So, first and foremost, I'm not going to focus on the businesses. The ecosystem is clearly centered around business.

From the advisory standpoint, there are investment banks that either have or do not have an equity stockbroking function inside them.

Since the early 1990s, these two activities have been linked, which may seem like ancient history to you, but it isn't to me.

Finally, these two parts have grown increasingly linked over time. So you've got investment banks, accounting and auditing firms that handle the financial diligence and accounting side of transactions.

The legal experts who handle the paperwork and documentation of the transactions, as well as consulting firms that may or may not be involved.

The larger the client firm, the more likely it is to be involved. From a strategic standpoint, from a due diligence standpoint, and from an international perspective, they're quite useful since they frequently have foreign offices.

If you work as an investment banking adviser, you must have a sector specialty.

Unless you're working in the tiniest of niches these days, being a generalist is hard.

That is my firm belief. I'm a Technology Specialist by trade. So, you must be familiar with the marketplace and its players, as well as various sub-sectors, how the industry is organized and structured, current trends, and driving forces propelling development in the sector.

Who are the key players and what are the most popular investments?

Then you'll need to have a thorough grasp of how to value firms in your sector. Because the methods and metrics used by different sectors to evaluate property firms differ, various industries employ distinct quantity systems and analysis approaches.

Let's have a look at the industry focus and extra information since you need to understand the company economic system.

What are the market's key participants?

It's crucial to recognize who the market leaders are, as well as which firms are expanding and who are threatening. And, honestly, do you have any idea who the targets are?

What are the organizations that your clients will be able to see as possible targets?

This list contains the names of private equity corporations and venture capital firms that may or may not be familiar to you. You should research who owns the businesses you're exploring.

It is simple to discover public businesses in most countries, but determining private firms depends on the area where you reside. It's quite simple in the United States and the United Kingdom.

More complicated information is more inaccessible in some European markets.

You'll also need to understand who all the venture capital and private equity firms are in the market, as well as which businesses they own and when they acquired them, so you can anticipate when they will exit them.

Are they buyers or consolidators? Are they growth firms or a target?

The majority of people would identify as a member of one or more of these cozy groups. But you only need to check out their recent history to see which category they fit in.

If you're an advisor, you'll need to understand the sector's deal history and who has done what in the past.

It's by paying attention to who is doing what to whom.

Then you may begin to assess possible possibilities from an advisory standpoint. However, because firms are continuously raising cash, the situation is complicated.

Many businesses come into existence daily. Companies that are making acquisitions and those who are divesting themselves from time to time abound.

If a firm goes from a private to a public company through an IPO, it now has paper that is publicly listed on which it may engage in acquisitions.

So they've effectively obtained an exit, but instead of morphing into a kind of business where they can now become an acquisition client, they've evolved into one that can.

You must first know who is financing the firms since you need to be sure they are viable.

You also need a strong national and global perspective since it's no longer enough to simply know what's going on in your market.

You must be aware of which firms are arriving from abroad to enter your market, or you must have a view on the businesses in your market who wish to expand overseas.

You may also provide them support as an advisor.

What is the most important question? The most important question is, from the sea of advisors and consultants; why should you be considered and hired?

You have the IBM issue stroke conundrum because no one has ever been disciplined for buying from them.

Clients will frequently prioritize working with large bulge bracket firms who are more likely to take them on, regardless of their experience.

But if you're not in a large firm, you'll have to be able to clearly distinguish your competitive advantage so that they see why they should want to hire you.

So you'll need a track record. You'll need to have closed deals. You'll need to be able to show your experience in the M&A process as well as in the sector.

You'll need to be able to start negotiations. You must be capable of coming up with creative ideas about firms that may be purchased for your client.

You need to be as specific as possible about how you'll be paid, whether you take a retainer, whether you work on a win-only basis, if you get compensated for phases, and whatever else is involved.

But you must make crystal clear what your business terms and conditions are.

So, if you decide to take that one, then you've got to determine who might be potential clients. So I'm now the investment banking advisor, and I'm planning my own marketing for my own firm.

So I need to be able to identify potential consumers. I'll want to build connections and contacts with the sellers. I'll want to know all of my sector's major financial investors.

You'll need to know who is conducting transactions, who has the money, and which businesses have access to cash.

You must also develop relationships with the decision-makers.

Let's talk about some of the outline abilities now: clearly, you'll need a thorough knowledge of the M&A procedure and the ability to distinguish between the buy and sell sides.

As a result, if you're on the buy side, you're working for a client who wants to acquire something.

If you're working for a client who wants to sell his firm, you're on the sell-side.

On the business' other side, consider what you'll do if you start a firm. You must be able to promote yourself. You must go out and market and persuade a customer to hire you in order for your company to succeed.

You'll also need to establish very explicit expectations for your customer. And that's usually done in the form of a lengthy engagement letter, which may contain many pages and often numerous more pages of boilerplate content.

Because it's critical to do so, you'll need to be able to communicate your skills and terms and conditions effectively.

Let's get down to business with our buy-side procedures. I've been engaged by a client to make an acquisition for them, so the first thing I must do is go through the sector and come up with potential targets for that customer.

The targets must be accessible. It's nice to have a paper exercise and a lengthy list of objectives, but it won't do you much good if the targets are hidden away.

Unless you know for certain that the board of that firm is ready to entertain a sale right now, it's pointless conversing with them.

Now, if they're talking about a deal in two years' time and you'll need to approach on behalf of your customer to find out if they're willing to have a conversation that leads to early discussions between the parties, which may or may not include your client and/or the disclosure of their name.

You might negotiate on a no-name basis. To begin with, you'll need to arrive at an agreement about value and valuation.

So you'll need to consult with the company's adviser and then communicate that view with your client.

As a result of our plan, we'll provide that value to the target company, which will eventually lead to negotiations. This results in the drafting of a letter of intent, which outlines the major conditions that will be negotiated.

You'll need to complete the remaining tasks, including arranging for a local consultant and insurance agent, conducting audits with your city's Environmental Health Department (E.H.D.) and other authorities if necessary, and submitting documentation of these activities to the bank as well as continuing to work in conjunction with them during the loan approval process.

Make sure there are no skeletons in the cupboard of the firm you're interested in purchasing. And then, at long last, everything is straightened out.

When you've completed the conditions, drawn up a sale and purchase contract, and agreed on the transaction on the sell-side as compared to when you're simply closing out your position.

You're back in the role of a buyer. You must persuade the client that you are capable of selling their business, just as the previous buyer did. As a result, you'll have to provide them with your thoughts on valuation and important terms that you believe would work for their company.

You'll also want to know what their main exit conditions are, as well as any other relevant information.

Does the management want to continue in the position?

Do they want to leave?

If you're thinking about selling your business to a foreign buyer, there are certain things you should speak with an attorney about. For example, finding out the market of potential purchasers, comprehending their strategy and why they do what they do will be crucial.

What you're seeking for is the acquirer that is prepared to pay a significant premium for your client and, as a result, obtain a higher price on exit than you would have otherwise.

The data room is the final portion of your due diligence, and it's where you'll place all of your company documentation. Accountants will be in charge of it, but at the end of the day, you are ultimately responsible as an investment banker for ensuring that it is completed.

Then you'll need to promote the business you want to sell. This is a solo rifle shot directed at one or two possible purchasers or a wide-reaching auction may be held, in which a variety of potential purchasers who are initially on a no-name basis, and who are only with a one or two-page teaser about the transaction.

But, once the potential buyer has expressed interest, you'll need an information memorandum for your marketing materials, which is generally a 30 or 40-page book about the firm that helps them form a viewpoint as to whether they want to make an offer.

After that, there will be bargaining and discussions, after which you'll receive an offer or multiple offers.

Those offers should ideally be negotiated and, eventually, terms agreed with a single buyer.

You may be discussing several hands terms at the same time, but you'll only want to join up with one that necessitates careful document preparation and results in final documentation seller puncher's contract closing and money transfer.

That is the second side of the agreement.

As a consultant, as an investment banker in this process, whether you need a lot of expertise. It's not something like an ethics kit building; this requires a lot of skill.

You'll need a network and contacts in your sector as well as across many financial investors and other investment banks.

You'll need a track record, as well as the ability to show your trustworthiness, because confidentiality and trust are essential.

To succeed in this industry, you must be able to sell your services and abilities to clients.

You'll need to be aware of how to promote their companies to other potential purchasers in the market.

You'll also need marketing abilities. You must master and comprehend all of the documentation.

You may not need to write much of it, but you'll want to be able to tell whether the sentence structure and weight of paragraphs and information in lengthy papers are correct and beneficial for your client.

You must be well-organized and in charge of the deal process since that's your primary responsibility.

That means following up on meetings, establishing meeting agendas, ensuring that action steps are completed, and ensuring that the process follows the timetable you established.

Of course, you'll need negotiation skills since you're the client's main negotiator and must advise them on how to structure the agreement and get it closed.

That's my personal viewpoint on mergers and acquisitions. I know this has been a long chapter, but I want to communicate my own experience with you so that you have faith in me when I say that I have a thorough knowledge of the mergers and acquisitions process.

Chapter 3: Overview of the Mergers and Acquisitions Process

To give you a high level overview of how the M&A process works, we'll spend some time looking at it in depth so you can understand the overall structure and flow of a transaction. This is all about providing you with a broad understanding of how the M&A procedure work.

Everything that I'm going to say after this will make sense if you have that framework.

It's critical to be clear when pitching a client, especially if you'll be giving him advice throughout the process.

That aids him in comprehending it since many times, if you're getting a new customer; they may not have gone through an M&A procedure before.

Similarly, you must manage their expectations about the intricacy and length of the project.

Let's start with step one, which is the acquisition plan. It's critical for your client or if you're the acquirer, yourself, to have a clear vision of what you want to buy.

What are you shooting for?

So, this isn't about the company's specifics. This is all about your company's long-term goals.

So we're talking about the markets here. Do you want to enter a new market or acquire some new items you can sell your current clients?

Do you want to explore new regions now? Regional geography may be one option, as could international geography.

Do you want to buy a competitor so you can expand your market share or get rid of some rivals so you can just raise your prices or have an easier battling road, especially if you've got someone who's rising up and may be a long-term danger to your company?

Step two is to fill in the search criteria, and here, the more information you can provide, the better.

The ideal firm, of course, does not exist in reality. From personal experience, I can tell you that firms often give me a long list of criteria to evaluate before they'll hire me. When I come back to them and tell them that the business does not exist, they may be shocked.

You're looking for a business that is scalable.

What is the company's revenue?

Where is it incorporated?

What kind of ownership does it have?

What's the company's position in the market?

Do you agree that your company is currently aligned with its overall brand?

So, that's what it boils down to.

You see, if you want to boost your market position, you must consider the region in which you're operating. Because if you're seeking to enhance your market position, of course, it's important.

What kind of people does the company serve? How large is their customer base?

What's the client mix like?

If your company has 80% of its sales going to one client, it's probably best to stay away.

And the organization's partners and suppliers are the World Health Organization. Of course, you'd have certain financial criteria in place, such as revenues, profits, cash flow, condition of the balance sheet, and of course, you'd be thinking about how to value and price these qualities.

With these methods in mind, define a target list of the companies you'd want to evaluate. Let's take a look at how we would value such an enterprise through some examples.

You may construct a long list of potential firms based on these criteria, so you can screen the market and look for all the businesses that meet your requirements equally, taking the information at hand you can navigate your way forward.

Let me give you an illustration.

A large public company in the United States planned to acquire an I.T. services firm in Germany that operated primarily within the SAP software ecosystem.

There were about 500 SAP partners in Germany at the time. After going through an exercise of screening those partners and shortlisting two options; essentially spoke with both firms, evaluated them, and decided to acquire one as a result.

But it's important to have a clear set of criteria and a clear acquisition scope that you can look at before going out and screening the market carefully so you don't waste your time looking for the other 499 companies.

The most essential part is to concentrate. A good criterion makes all the difference.

The fourth stage is to initialize. So you've compiled a short list of companies, and you go to see them. You begin conversations.

Now, you may either take on the role of an advisor on a no-names basis, keeping your customer in the shadows, or if you're dealing with things directly, you might start a discussion with the business owners trying to determine whether those firms are actually the sort of businesses you want to buy.

You're obviously seeking for knowledge. If the situation progresses, you will most certainly sign a confidentiality agreement; however, if it does not, you are merely attempting to get a feel for the company.

Is this a company that you think it is? And, more importantly, how interested are the firm's owners in selling it?

Now, at the conclusion, I'll make a key point, but you should really attempt to discover why the proprietors/directors or owners want to sell their business.

It's also possible that for their own personal reasons, which may be retirement or any other activities they've got going on in their lives, they want to move on to something new.

The company is poised to collapse. And one of the businesses we studied in the United States was precisely the problem. We consistently received a different set of statistics and they were worse than those before when we last reviewed them.

So, you must understand the seller's motivation. But, equally, if the seller has no incentive to sell, they are more likely to accept a bargain.

If you offer them a really high pie in the sky price, which is far more than you want to spend. However, if they don't have a desire to sell, it's probably not the best moment to focus on them and try to locate someone who wants or needs to sell.

You've now arrived at a valuation phase, which is step 5. To arrive at a sensible value for the company, you'll need thorough and current information on it, as well as financial data.

You'll need to get the information from the business's executives.

If you want to keep the information they provided under wraps, you'll need a confidentiality agreement in writing. It's also beneficial if you can obtain their year-end budget so that you have an idea of where things are heading for the company.

If you're performing an appraisal, one of the things you'll most likely want to do is construct your own forecasts for the company and get management input on them. That's really useful.

Value the firm on its own. What is the value of a company when it is alone? They're selling what the sellers are offering, after all.

You can consider the advantages to you of acquiring the firm in your valuation, but these are frequently referred to as synergies.

However, you won't pay for those perks. As a result, you want to understand what the advantages will be and what the increase in value will be after you purchase.

However, you want to value the firm on a stand-alone basis since that's what the sellers are offering and, of course, use a variety of valuation methods. Look at comparable numbers, P.E. ratios of public firms, and other transactions that have taken place in the market.

The value of the company will also be influenced by who owns it. And I mean in terms of public companies, you'll have to pay a premium above and beyond what's available on the market if it's a corporation.

If it's a private firm, the owners may not be as sophisticated, and they may be prepared to accept a lower price if venture capitalists or private equity firms are involved. They'll be more tough and seasoned negotiators if that's the case because they'll view their exit value solely in terms of the returns to their funds, so you might consider hiring an experienced negotiator.

Step six is where the hard work begins. It's time to negotiate the contract to the point where you can sign a letter of intent and MOU.

You've gone from sending a letter to two or three companies, to having detailed discussions with probably just two or three businesses in order to get down to the nitty gritty details of what kind of deal you can put together, what sort of offer, what sort of number, and so on.

What you're attempting to do here is list the most essential parts of the transaction that are important to the seller.

Because when you negotiate the fine details of the agreement, if you understand what matters most to them, it's much simpler to trade off points and acquire the points in the deal that you want in return for addressing some of their concerns.

You want to get to the point where you have a non-binding letter of intent, which lays out the main points of the agreement.

Everybody agrees to that, and they all sign up for it.

The seventh stage is the due diligence phase, which might take up to six weeks. It's a comprehensive examination of all parts of the business and the obtaining of this data will result in thorough information requests from you and your advisors.

It's critical that they have a data room where they've organized all of this corporate company information in an easy-to-search manner, and it's being systematically filed. Today, this is very much an online process.

So all the information should be accessible, and once you've been given access to it, you should be able to answer the questions that you have.

Normally, a due diligence review is carried out by professionals such as accountants, attorneys, managers, and so on.

It's a lot of effort, but it's not difficult to comprehend. It is also an opportunity to really get into the company and learn everything there is to know about it. That's the goal of the exercise.

So you're looking for some of these things, and in order to verify your viewpoint on the company's value, you'll have to look through the business's details, especially its financial data.

The key to this is transparency. You want the sellers to reveal anything outstanding or awful about the company. You want to know where all of the skeletons are buried.

Clearly, you'll be concerned about the company's finances. You'll consider the firm's assets and liabilities. The facilities may be viewed. You'll examine the client's clients and suppliers. You'll look at all of the contracts with people who work for or deal with the client, from vendors to customers to employees.

They've got an agreement with the landowner or property owners, whether it's a contract for entering into. You also need to understand the contracts they sell their goods and services under in order to fully comprehend.

Are they selling at a similar rate to you and in the same contracts? One of the most important factors to consider is change of control provisions, which may contain things like a right of termination if there's a takeover.

And if they exist, you must discover them. Finally, of course, you must examine all the various personal difficulties, management, and staff to ensure that nothing is overlooked.

That is only a short description of all the problems. The due diligence process, data requests, and other procedures can be extremely time-consuming. In this brief chapter, I can't possibly go into all the specifics.

In step eight, we're talking about the contract for sale and purchase. This is something you should complete in conjunction with the due diligence procedure.

It begins on the basis of a letter of intent, which is one element of why you have a letter of intent.

The first step towards drafting the purchase agreement is completed. Obviously, there are several conditions in the seller purchase agreement that must be negotiated.

You must provide comprehensive information, and you must make certain representations and warranties. Your legal staff will inform you on the details of these legal documents.

However, the important thing is to have as much information from the sellers as possible so that you are fully informed about the company.

The working capital agreement will have to be negotiated. And I don't want to go into detail, but the firm must be allowed enough cash for it to operate effectively.

Normally, you wouldn't be able to let the sellers take out all of the money and then discover that you don't have enough cash in your firm to pay the staff.

Working capital is an extremely vital negotiation. And there are always a lot of other contracts, reports, and shareholder agreements in addition to the purchase agreement if the seller maintains a position in the firm or has a financial interest in it.

So you've got all of these additional reports and agreements that arrive in tandem.

You've got a 150 - page contract for the sale and purchase, but there are also numerous ancillary contracts and other disclosures strewn across the table because it's all part of the sale and purchase agreement.

It's a time-consuming procedure.

The final stage is acquisition finance. You'll have known you could pay for it or how you'd pay for it going into the agreement.

But this is the area in the agreement where finance becomes involved. As a result, you must also plan ahead of time.

You may be performing it from existing sources, such as a company that has a lot of cash on its balance sheet and is willing to pay out of cash or with stock.

Not too difficult. If you're talking about a private-company to-private-company conversion, it's not that difficult.

If it's a public company, you'll have to go through a formal share distribution procedure, making things more difficult.

Understand how the transaction will be paid for either cash shares or whatever else it is. And, if you'll need to do any fundraising or debt repayment, make sure everything's on track.

Step ten, following up and closing the transaction. Fermentation is not a component of the M&A process, but it's the next step that we all go into a room to discuss things.

The cork is removed and the champagne is poured, at which time some money passes from one bank to another, the consideration passes between parties, or shares are delivered to sellers.

After that, everyone else who is still in the company will presumably need to follow up on the post-deal implementation plan, which they will have been planning for weeks.

So you'll know on day one that you're joining a new firm or the company that's being bought, and you'll make the announcement to staff. You'll know exactly what actions you'll take in the following day, few days, week, and weeks.

So it's a time-consuming but critical operation. But in this series of chapters, I'm not going to dive into the intricacies of post-acquisition implementation.

To summarize, the M&A process is straight forward if you have a firm grasp on the fundamentals. It does follow a logical and sequential path, but it is complicated, requiring intricate transaction management, which is why experience in this sector is crucial.

It's much easier if you can anticipate issues before they happen, and that requires experience.

Keep in mind that deals might come to an end at any moment for a variety of reasons. You could have market conditions, the buyer backing out, or the seller withdrawing.

You can have something showing up in due diligence that is a deal breaker. You may have someone putting up a condition that is a deal breaker, as well as altering the price, which is also a deal-breaker.

So, as a result, it becomes quite a tough job, and it's a real personnel and management problem. The greater you can develop the connection between the buyer and the seller, the more likely the arrangement will come to pass.

The key, in my opinion, is to make sure the seller has a compelling reason to want to sell rather than just wanting to sell to your buyer. They may walk away at any time without that crucial incentive.

Consider it in any transaction you do, and look for individuals who are highly motivated to sell.

That concludes our tour of the M&A process.

I've provided you a lot of information, but I hope the structure makes it simple to understand and adhere to. And, as we'll discuss now, everything we're going on about will become clear.

Section 2 | What does the Term Mergers and Acquisitions Mean?

Chapter 4: What does the Term Mergers and Acquisitions Mean - Overview?

What exactly do we mean by the phrase "mergers and acquisitions," which is something that has been in popular usage for at least 20 or 30 years, and which you hear discussed in the news and in business on a daily basis?

But what exactly does the phrase or the term "M &A" imply? In broad terms, we're talking about the mix of companies or business assets. So, when you combine two of these three things, you get either a merger or an acquisition. Now, there are several sorts of agreements, and I don't want to get too technical right away.

In general, you can have a merger in which two firms are roughly equivalent. Companies combine and combine. You may obtain an acquisition in which one firm takes control of another.

A consolidation is possible. This is when a firm goes out and gathers up a slew of little businesses. So it's consolidating a fragmented market in order to get one dominant player who aims to dominate the sector.

Under the circumstances, opposition to a tender offer can come from numerous areas. A public company or privately-held firm might make a tender offer for the shares of a publicly listed firm, and they may do so if it's hostile, circumventing management of the target organization by offering cash or their own shares in order to take control of and acquire it.

You can have asset purchases, and this involves the acquisition of a company's assets. A firm may be acquired without itself being purchased.

There's a substantial distinction to consider when it comes to goodwill, because if you acquire the assets, you can leave behind all of the liabilities in the company that you're targeting.

However, the organizations that make up the company may be divided and purchased into another business entity.

Then we get into the realm of management purchases or buyouts, where a financial investor, usually backed by a group of senior executives, enters another firm and takes control.

So those are the most frequent types of M&A transactions.

We've already covered this in some detail, but we'll go into it in much more depth throughout this book.

Chapter 5: What Separates a Merger from an Acquisition?

It's critical to grasp this, since these phrases are frequently confused with one another as if they meant the same thing.

In simple terms, they are quite different. A merger is a situation in which two businesses of comparable size join forces to form a new joint business.

In theory, both may be considered equals. And that's why such combinations are sometimes referred to as a merger of equals.

The most frequent situation is to see the board's major duties evenly distributed among the members.

If one firm provides the chairman, another might provide the CEO.

There are times when there is a combined CEO appointment, but these are uncommon.

So it's really a collaboration of two businesses. The enterprises decide to collaborate with one another as part of the agreement.

Although the sums are comparable, there is often a lot of bargaining regarding the terms of the agreement. There will be a lot of battling for the ideal share of value.

It's unusual for the split to be exactly 50/50. It might be 60 40 or 55 45, but one side is always attempting to gain an advantage over the other.

Then, both sets of shareholders must sign off on the merger. When the transaction is complete, the two firms are combined into a new corporate entity.

This is usually done by creating a new CEO at the top, who then takes control of businesses and their day-to-day operations, as well as systems and everything else.

When two businesses combine, it is often difficult to identify the difference between them. A good example of this is when Chrysler and Daimler Benz combined to form Chrysler Daimler. A terrific example of this is when a firm combines its operations with those of another company.

That was genuinely a merger of equals. When, in reality, a deal is referred to as a merger rather than an acquisition, it's usually because the acquirer intends to purchase the target company.

The primary cause for this is to allow the purchasing firm to present the agreement as a more friendly offer to target company shareholders and management.

So, they're telling people that it's a merger and putting it forward in the open as if it were a combine, when in fact the buyer is acquiring and taking over the target.

When one firm acquires another, what exactly do we mean by an acquisition?

Now, a lot of the time, this is a major business acquiring a smaller one, but when this happens, no new firm is formed.

A takeover occurs when a buyer purchases the target company and absorbs it, often known as "acquisition."

The acquiring firm purchases a controlling interest or sometimes up to 100% of the target company.

The target business does not alter its name or corporate structure, but it becomes a completely owned subsidiary of the entity that acquired it.

Now, the operations are handled from there by the business, however in legal terms, the target firm has disappeared below the corporate entity and ownership of the purchasing corporation.

An acquisition might now be purchased for cash, stock, or a combination of both.

Occasionally, you'll find more complex designs, lower notes, buyouts, and a variety of other features.

But essentially the exchange is cash or paper in return for the business and assets of the target company.

So, in order to grasp the distinctions between a merger and an acquisition, it's crucial to understand what the nuances of that distinction are. The first is that there's a big difference between them.

Chapter 6: Why Do Businesses Merge?

Let's consider why businesses merge.

We know that a merger is the result of two companies agreeing to combine, and this usually implies the formation of a new corporate entity as a consequence.

Why do they feel the need to?

What are the reasons for companies to merge?

Basically, there are a few fundamental reasons for this. First and foremost, it's the chance to branch out into new products or geographic markets.

As a result, one firm's product may be the other firm's missing ingredient; one business may be operating in a geographic market that the other does not.

It's a way to grab market share. If two businesses operate in the same sector and join forces, their market share will rise.

Diversify doesn't have to be a bad thing. It can even help them develop faster than that when used together. It's an opportunity to get rid of duplicate expenditures and eliminate overlap from the company.

These are known as synergy.

There are a number of advantages to be gained by combining two firms and then eliminating the overlap.

It's a chance to expand income. The hypothesis is that if you combine these two firms, the rejuvenation of the businesses with the extra energy and new ideas and larger products and service offers, they'll be able to sell more products to the same consumers, therefore growing revenues and profits.

Finally, all of this is about, of course, generating value for shareholders. This is simply what it's all been about since the beginning.

Now, there are five primary sorts of business mergers to consider, and I'd want to go through each one with you. In turn, they are conglomerate CN, generic or generic market extension, horizontal and vertical conglomerates.

Let's start with the big example. These are where two completely unrelated firms operate in distinct industries, in separate geographic locations, and pursue to capture the entire market.

You are working to gain a product or market expansion. This was a very popular tactic in the 1970s, when it was claimed that expert management could run any sort of company.

The more businesses you gave to highly effective management, the greater value you created as a result of their being superior than other managers by integrating your lower overhead.

The issue, though, is that management expertise has become the baseline discussion. Despite its age, this argument remains popular among investors today. It was the primary reason behind the 60s and early 70s epidemic of mergers and acquisitions.

The next approach is called horizontal integration, and it's when two firms operate in the same market and are simply selling competing goods with an aim of increasing their product range by merging.

This is frequently the case, which means that it necessitates cross-functional collaboration. It entails overlapping market marketing, manufacturing operations, R&D, and product lines from different firms being combined.

So, if your firm sells washing machines and another firm sells vacuum cleaners, you can sell washers and vacuums to the same consumer by combining the two.

By implementing these techniques, you may potentially expand your income and sales while also expanding market share.

A global market extension is a technique of expanding the reach of one's market by combining businesses that offer similar products but operate in different areas.

It's simple. A horizontal integration occurs when firms in the same field merge to sell comparable goods to one another, resulting in lower prices and increased competitiveness.

In the banking industry, for example, you see enormous banks merging, and they're essentially selling the same sets of products and services.

They have an M&A department, a bond department, and an equity department. They have a consumer goods, financial services division.

They do this by combining them with one another, and they're going for economies of scale and market share.

It's become a horizontal combination, and it's now a vertical combination; component businesses now provide component parts or services across an industry, but at distinct levels in the supply chain.

Consider an example from the oil sector. So you might have an oil refining company, as well as an oil sales and distribution firm. Maybe they own forecourts or a firm that sells refined oils produced at refineries to marketplaces.

However, if you combine those two things together, they may provide that one service. They can handle the refinement and distribution of the product to the client base.

This frequently provides financial and operational synergies.

You take out the margin between the two firms since the top company, the refining firm, will want to sell its goods and services to the distribution firm with a product attachment.

If you combine those factors, the profit has been subtracted from the middle and they may more successfully sell their firm's products at the other end to that conclusion, consumers.

Vertical combinations are emerging as a way for businesses to compete by offering products and services from the same sector, yet at varying stages in the supply chain.

As a result, those are the reasons for corporate marriages. If you're looking at a business agreement, you may often look at it and say, "Well, yes," because the rationale provided for the deal makes it very clear why it's taking place.

Chapter 7: Why Do Organizations Make Acquisitions?

Let's look at why businesses buy each other, since we already know that taking control of another firm is how acquisitions happen.

This is generally done by acquiring more than 50% of the firm's shares.

We won't go into the gory details of share ownership structures that include numerous classes of shares.

The takeover is defined by the financial control of the target firm's equity. And this is generally seen with major businesses acquiring tiny corporations.

That's the typical pattern for a takeover. However, you may also have a situation where a little firm acquires an enormous one, and that's known as a reverse acquisition.

The most common reason is that the small firm is a public company and the BIG business is a private entity.

This allows the larger private company to go public without having to go through the full IPO process.

Now, let's look at some of the reasons why businesses combine two entities to increase their size and gain economies of scale.

So, because of this, costs may be reduced across the combined business, however most often the expenditures are removed from the acquired firm and little else is altered in the buyer's structure.

Purchasing a competitor can provide the buyer greater market share. So if they buy a company that already has 10% of the market and they have 10%, the target's share is 5%.

They might capture 15% of the market, if not more. The synergy advantages are frequently mentioned as compelling reasons to go ahead with the transaction.

This is a comprehensive description of the cost savings that can be enjoyed by the business as well as some of the growth advantages that may be obtained through integration.

These are often discussed, but they seldom perform as intended.

Synergies must be examined with caution and not taken for granted. The buyer may get the chance to enter a certain market through acquisitions.

Now, this might be a new product or a new market. It may be in the United States. It could move from the West Coast to the East Coast, but also from the United States to Europe.

That's not necessarily the case. In reality, generating a deal for market entrance is an excellent motivation to do so. It's also an opportunity for product or technology, IP or technical knowledge, and other things to be obtained.

You'll see this in most of the large tech firms, including Google, Facebook, and Microsoft. They're frequently buying little, innovative technology companies for their technologies, research, and intellectual property and patents.

On the West Coast, in fact. These huge internet businesses frequently find that acquiring a group of knowledgeable engineers is simpler than trying to recruit a team or individuals separately.

In such a competitive market, scarcity of outstanding talent is one of the major problems. As a result, these are all factors that motivate businesses to make acquisitions.

What differentiates a "Takeover" from an "Acquisition"?

To put it another way, takeovers and acquisitions are the same thing; however, a takeover has negative connotations, whereas an acquisition implies that the target firm has consented to be taken over by the larger firm.

Frequently, hostile transactions and amiable deals are discussed.

What does this signify? A hostile takeover is a situation in which the buyer must persuade the target company's stockholders to sell their shares, despite the fact that the target company's managers do not wish to make a deal.

You'll also notice these changing in corporate board meetings, which is understandable since the shareholders and management are often two separate teams.

The firm has gone public and is now listed on the stock market. The management has a small portion of the company's shares, due to which they are able to control it.

As a result, the buyer can appeal to the shareholders over the management company's head if they control or own more than 50 percent of the equity.

This may happen in public firms as well. However, it's rare and unusual.

This can happen after an initial offering, but after a period of time, the original investors' stakes will be diluted or they will sell.

If the management team controls 50 percent, they aren't put in danger of being taken over in a hostile takeover because all they have to do is say no.

The arrangement has to be beneficial for both sides. The buyer must persuade them to sell their assets.

So, in hostile deals, that's the distinction between a bad and good bargain.

There's an increased amount of management and regulation throughout the duration of the transaction due to the conflict.

That's true in the United States, too; and the takeover panel manages it in the United Kingdom.

What does it mean for a company to be "accretive" or "dilutive"?

This is another phrase that's frequently used in connection with acquisition. It's a dilutive or accretive deal, and it adds to the buying firm's earnings per share. A dilutive transaction, on the other hand, reduces the earnings per share of the acquiring company.

However, bear in mind that accretion and dilution are not static; they can change over time, and the management will frequently claim that a deal will become accretive as synergies are produced and additional growth is achieved.

This is just a sample of the reasons behind acquisitions, and I hope it provides some perspective into why businesses want to make purchases.

Chapter 8: What exactly do we mean by "Synergies"?

What exactly do you mean by synergies in a merger and acquisition transaction? Synergies are a catchall phrase for the advantages that exist when two business enterprises are combined.

Now, sometimes these are only short, and other times they're more imagined than real.

You'll get the top executives from one or both sides releasing lengthy reports and statements outlining the wonderful potential of this corporate merger and why they're going to be able to create so many synergy effects and much shareholder value.

Because synergies are frequently overlooked, they are commonly accused of being deceptive. However, it's critical to comprehend what they're and where they might originate.

So, what exactly are synergies?

What exactly does this phrase imply?

Essentially, there are two sides to the discussion. There is a chance for revenue growth as well as a chance for cost savings.

Either of these, on the other hand, unquestionably has a beneficial influence on the company's earnings.

In the most basic sense, therefore, synergies may be achieved since there is more development.

When two firms are combined, you would anticipate the resulting entity to provide more chances and for the organizations to develop quicker and deeper. They've got consumer bases they can address now.

They've got goods and services and technology, among other things. As a result, the company should be able to expand more quickly, acquire new clients, and improve profit margins, and so on.

This is the most inclusive definition of synergy, but we may be more particular.

Let's begin with competition, and an acquisition or merger may prevent a rival from obtaining the same deal's benefits.

So it improves the buyer's or enlarged firm's competitive position, depending on whether you're talking about a purchase or a merger.

In a highly competitive market, scarcity of targets may make this a critical consideration since if you can retain the services of those individuals in that technology for your company, you're preventing a competitor from obtaining it.

Another example is the acquisition of Oculus by Facebook, which occurred before the company had any revenues. Rather than waiting for a company to generate a profit and acquire customers, Facebook swooped in and acquired it preemptively. Acquisitions are frequently costly, but it's possible to invest beforehand to decrease the cost of acquiring them. Investing money upfront for this strategy is often called "pre-acquisition investment."

That was to restrict access to that knowledge and prevent others from obtaining it.

A company combination or acquisition can help a company achieve or enhance its market leadership.

If you have market leadership, you can begin to lay down sector rules.

You have the ability to overpower with your size and scale, which can provide you with a variety of other advantages.

Of course, there are monopolies that are carefully watched in the United States and across Europe as well as elsewhere throughout the world.

A combination of tax benefits, on the other hand, may be used to achieve market leadership or a step towards it.

I'm not a tax expert. And I'm not shelling out Tax advice. Please consult with your attorneys and CPA, when you act on your learning.

However, one of the methods that U.S. firms have been employing is to acquire a foreign firm in a low-tax jurisdiction because corporate tax rates in the United States were some of the highest in the world, and to shelter some of their US domiciled earnings via various perfectly acceptable tax avoidance strategies through this combination.

Now, President Trump has lowered US corporate tax rates at the end of last year, suggesting that this may no longer be a viable approach.

Reducing expenses is a natural fit. When two firms join forces, there will be overlap in personnel, particularly in the core business processes such as marketing, sales, accounting, H.E.R., and so on. There's going to be duplication in those areas.

Only one head of marketing is required; however, you may have many heads of H.R., as long as they are all different individuals. Duplication might result in a decrease in personnel costs, which is clearly beneficial.

Occasionally, it includes the mother board as well. You don't need two CEOs in a merger, but you may have one guy who becomes chair, the other guy becomes CEO, and so on.

Sometimes, they will be rewarded handsomely for quitting the firm. Thank you very much.

However, these advantages in terms of personnel overlap may provide serious financial advantages for big business economies of scale if properly utilized.

You can't build your own supplier engine from the ground up. However, you may be able to find suppliers who will give better terms and margins, be able to work for higher margins, and price more effectively.

As a result, they obtain benefits just from their size, which should influence the bottom line.

There are also advantages that are somewhat more subjective, yet nonetheless quite apparent through the acquisition of items like technology, business procedures, and expertise in intellectual property, and technical skills.

This implies that quantifying these advantages might be more challenging at times.

But, if you're a fast-growing technology firm looking for specialists in virtual reality like the one that Facebook purchased, then there are few options. If you can't hire these individuals individually to form your own team, the best approach is to purchase them.

That is a clear synergy.

Typically, you'll get the knowledge and expertise you need at a lower rate.

Oculus Rift is more of a technical IP deal than simply a personal abilities and specialist experts bargain, as it contains far more technology than was required for the initial development.

To sum it up, I'd want to say that there was a difference between owing someone money or owing them something. -> To summarize, I'm sure you can grasp what I'm attempting to express.

A third aspect is brand recognition and exposure. I'm not talking about wasting money here. There's a saying in marketing that goes, "Never put all of your eggs in one basket." That's because if the firm becomes a market leader, the brand gets more recognized and it becomes easier to attract new consumers.

They have more resources, which may help them to improve their marketing and distribution.

It's also possible that they have a greater understanding of marketing, which might lead to new sales possibilities.

Furthermore, large businesses may benefit from funding since they are considered less risky than smaller firms by nature.

That concludes our discussion of the financial synergies that might emerge from a partnership, merger, or acquisition.

You'll notice that it's a somewhat subjective topic. It's always intriguing to go through and see what synergies a company is claiming, especially if the premium paid to finance the transaction is justifiable.

Chapter 9: What are the Role of Advisory in the Mergers and Acquisitions Market?

Let's have a look at who the advisory players are in the mergers and acquisitions market now.

There are various consulting firms that operate in this sector and have varied roles and responsibilities, as well as competence.

Also, bear in mind that every transaction has two sides: a seller and a buyer.

Because you have two sets of advisors on both sides, but they will have different responsibilities and you may not get them mirrored on the other side.

Let me explain. The primary and most important player in this market is without a doubt the investment banks.

The investment banks are the ones who are considered to be calling the shots most of the time because they have closest relationships with the businesses that are out there creating and executing deals.

Now, their responsibilities will be many, with the first of them being to underwrite the loan.

What this essentially implies is that the lender provides the buyer with the assurance that money will be accessible by stating if we can't raise it, we'll give it from our own resources.

The term "underwriting" refers to the process of evaluating a person's credit situation and determining whether or not he or she is qualified for a loan.

You may now take a risk with other gamers instead of the banks, allowing them to avoid actually having to pay out the cash.

The bottom line is that the buyer must be informed he can pay the amount of money required by the target company, and they must know they will be paid if they accept this method.

There must be confidence that the funds will be available.

If the company needs to raise money through a share issue or a debt issue, banks will confirm that they can accomplish it and guarantee it because they'll underwrite it.

They'll also be a financial consultant.

These men will take charge of the entire process, but they will particularly advise you on financing.

It's possible that they're an investment banker. So, if there's a share issue or if the company is being acquired, their equity teams will be handling the situation of new shares and purchasing existing shares from the target corporation.

The number of hours worked by this role will vary depending on the needs of the client. They'll advise on deal structure and pricing, but it goes further since they'll manage the whole investment process, so they'll help with target identification.

They'll assist the buyer in coming up with and agreeing to a fair valuation and price, typically by producing a detailed and complicated document that goes through each of the different valuation techniques and rates the target, after which you will consider the premium.

It's a role that involves gathering all the paperwork, from confidentiality agreements and letters of intent to managing, but not necessarily drafting the closing documents.

They'll be in charge of the process, so they'll be organizing meetings, the timetable, and the rest of the players, as well as attorneys, accountants, and other advisors throughout the process.

The company's vice president of finance will host the meeting, which will be attended by other members of the senior leadership team.

However, once you're done with the meeting, they'll sit there with their list of priorities and make sure that everything is covered. They will also follow up on any topics that may have been missed during the meeting.

They will play an important role in the negotiation from their clients' standpoint, especially when it comes to contracts.

So they will lead. While it may be appealing to let your financial advisor take the lead and you sit back as the main, this is not always the case. While your adviser fights for you, you can argue from a reserved position and he or she will have to return to get clearance from you before proceeding; however, much of the closing documentation is written by lawyers.

Let's speak about the attorneys for a moment. The law firms primarily handle legal documentation for the transaction, ranging from confidentiality agreements to sale and purchase contracts.

They'll also be responsible for conducting legal due diligence, which is the process of examining the target company's legal status.

They'll go through all of their contracts, employment contracts, and supply agreements. They'll even look at incorporation papers and other corporate paperwork.

They checked to see whether their leases were in order and that everything from a legal standpoint was correct, and they're willing to go through it all again if need be.

Of course, if it's a cross-border transaction, you're talking about two sets of law, two sets of different rules and regulations that must be followed.

And, of course, the huge law firms have. Both jurisdictions claim to have relevant experience in both bodies of law and are able to provide that assistance.

The audit and accounting firms take care of the financial side, with lawyers handling the legal side. On the target firm, the audit and accounting firms will be in charge of financial and accounting due diligence.

They will be given the opportunity to have a say in the valuation. There's always a negotiation about how much money is available for working capital.

They will also look at tax concerns from the perspective of both the target company and the deal's structure.

And, of course, cross-border concerns add to the complexity of the financial issue, especially when it comes to tax.

They will then be able to have a voice in it as well. Management consulting firms, as we said, are businesses that provide advisory services or consultative services.

They're the ones who are most engaged in strategy. They aren't always around if they have a job.

However, the major corporations will undoubtedly pay attention and converse with consulting firms to obtain a perspective and offer suggestions on their plan.

They'll also be giving you strategy advice. They'll be identifying and assessing targets.

They may well be conducting company due diligence, visiting businesses and creating an audit diligence report on the management and the company.

They may even have a say in the valuation of your business.

So those are the key advisory players in this process, and they're surrounded by a network of other players. The buyer sits in the middle.

Naturally, you'll have your own team of advisors on the other side. On that side, you'll also have a target and a target will have its own set of counselors.

And that's what the advisory players' ecosystem appears to be.

Chapter 10: Financing an Acquisition through Capital Raising

I'd like to go through acquisition finance now so that you may have a better idea of where your company's capital will come from.

Clearly, acquisitions and merger transactions must be financed.

This is frequently the duty of the advising investment bank.

Who is advising the buyer?

The primary purpose of the corporate finance advisor is to arrange the acquisition financing.

They also get paid a commission for arranging the funding and other advisory services.

Financing can be done with equity or debt, as well as combinations of the two and variants of the two.

Things tend to get really complicated; but let's just try and keep it basic for the time being, and concentrate on the fundamentals.

A contract may be paid for using almost solely money or stock, with paper, and even equity.

If you have cash to reinvest, it can come from bank debt and loans, or it could be in the form of money that's already been kept within the business.

Of course, you can subsequently mix debt and equity financing to pay for part of the purchase price with cash and part of it with equity.

A debt finance arrangement might include a variety of loans with varying durations.

In order to close a significant transaction, several layers of various tranches of debt are frequently utilized, which may be sold to various sorts of investors to assemble the whole package.

These are generally known as senior, junior, and mezzanine.

The senior debt has the lowest coupon, is the most secure, and has the greatest call on assets against which it is secured.

Senior debt is safer than junior debt, despite the fact that it has a greater chance of default.

In the event of liquidation, it pays a greater coupon and is ranked below senior.

Then mezzanine is almost a kind of mix between debt and equity, with the lowest call on the assets but the highest risk.

All of these various risk profiles and coupon payment profiles are attractive to various types of investors.

So, where can you get your cash from?

So, clearly, you may acquire the assets that the buyer has to begin with.

So they may already have cash on the books or they might utilize their paper to acquire it.

They can do it by issuing new shares to their existing shareholders for cash and then using the money to make the acquisition.

They can go to banks and request that they lend them money, and the banks will provide the package once they are organized.

This is the investment bank, and they'll do it in whatever form of financing package turns out to be most beneficial.

The difficulties we've already addressed. Then, third, you can go to private equity firms, venture capital businesses that will invest in the company and lend money to complete the transaction.

The majority of these events are referred to as buyout transactions, but I don't want to get too technical.

Consider the many ways to finance and acquire when you're learning about the fundamentals of financing and acquisition.

So, that's a very brief overview. However, if you start to consider where the money will come from, then we're starting to move forward in our understanding of how mergers and acquisitions operate.

Chapter 11: How Are Companies Valued in the M&A Market?

What role does the purchase of a company play in mergers and acquisitions? In a merger, both sides claim that their company's worth is greater than that of the other.

The reason for this is that when you combine the two firms, they're squabbling over the portion of the pie.

They will want to dispute that their valuation is, for example, $1 billion. And the other company's value is half a billion dollars.

As a result, they obtain two-thirds of the increased pie twice as big in the acquisition.

The buyer is looking to pay as little as feasible while the seller is seeking to get the greatest possible price.

The buyer will come up with a target's worth and submit an offer.

The buyer may also rely on a common argument: that the target firm is being undervalued and that the buyer must pay more for them because their valuation is higher.

That's all there is to it. There are just two main ways to do it.

There are numerous alternative methods. But let's stick to these two major approaches for the time being.

The first is referred to as comparable transactions, and the second is known as discounted cash flow.

Let's examine comparable transactions. Comparables can be utilized in acquisitions by comparing similar market transactions and determining the metrics on which the total deal consideration was paid.

So you're looking at a business deal that's occurred in the market, and it's been announced, as well as the company's revenues and profits.

You'll have a better grasp of the company's value. You'll know how much was paid for each item. And with that in mind, you've got the whole deal's structure.

They want to know how much debt the company has. As a result, you obtain an enterprise value rather than an equity value.

Then you add metrics to those values, such as the price-to-earnings ratio, which examines the value of a business as a multiple of its earnings per share.

Once you've calculated the earnings per share ratio for a number of companies, it's common to aggregate them and take averages.

So you have a wide range of possibilities, from high to low. You may eliminate any unusual figures since no two businesses are alike.

So, to compare the company's sales to its income ratio with the organization's sales to earnings (SAR) ratio, you'll need more than one.

There are many of them, but I'm only going to focus on a few. This is essentially how much the company is worth as a multiple of sales.

If a company is still in its early phases and has yet to produce profits, this may be quite beneficial.

This is a more involved procedure in discounted cash flow, but essentially what you're proposing is that we value the target firm today on the basis of a valuation. This represents the future cash flows that we think this business will produce in the coming years, including a terminal Valuation at the end.

We'll use the weighted average cost of capital for that firm as a discount factor to bring these future cash flows back to the present day.

So you project the value based on future cash flows, which are then discounted to the present and summed up.

You execute this ad infinitum for five or ten years since you can't go on like that forever.

Then, at the end of that time period, you have a terminal value, which you then discount to today's dollars to obtain a discounted cash flow valuation of the target firm.

Furthermore, there's the issue of an acquisition premium.

The premium is the most important component of a forward price option, and it's also known as the "worth to justify" or "justification value." This is what you have to pay in addition to the share's value in order for the selling shareholders to agree that they should sell their shares.

What incentive do the target shareholders have to sell their shares if you're going to pay the present value of the business?

That is not the case. As a result, you must add a premium to the company's stock market value when you compute it.

This is the "windfall" component. It's the largest component, representing any and all cash gains that might be expected as a result of future growth. In addition, there are many other financial elements involved in this calculation that we won't go over here. And they're all related to one another!

This will also entice them to sell their shares since they won't be able to work with you anymore.

That is a beginning look at how valuing enters into mergers and acquisitions, and how firms and their advisors go about estimating the targets that they want to purchase.

Chapter 12: The Mergers and Acquisitions Market

I'd like to walk you through a typical merger and acquisition process. Now, there are differences between private agreements and public agreements, but the general procedure is the same.

The rules are similar, however the nitty-gritty details vary.

Let's get this party started. And a board has determined that it wishes to make an acquisition or merge with another firm for business reasons, which we can understand because we've looked at why firms want to acquire and combine businesses.

So the first step is to assess the possibilities. And this entails looking at the competitors in their industry and assessing them against a plan they wish to follow, as well as identifying objectives and selecting a goal.

They'll most likely choose two or three targets and investigate them simultaneously.

If it's a public company that they're after and they're a public company, they'll almost certainly attempt to acquire a tiny number of shares on the open market before having to declare.

They can now buy up to 5% of a company's equity in the United States before having to notify the FCC and make an affirmation.

There are also regulations in the UK market to prevent investors from being snuck up on.

I believe the percentage is about three percent in the United Kingdom, where you must disclose a major stake and, if the firm reaches its goal, whether or not it gets wind that someone is establishing a position in it. It has the capacity to approach them and ask them to reveal their share publicly.

When they get to that point, they've built a five percent stake and must declare their shareholdings publicly and state their intentions—whether they intend to purchase the firm or maintain their investment.

Clearly, if it's a private agreement, there is no church stake building; nevertheless, they will contact the target firm.

The buyer, the firm looking to make the acquisition, or the merger will now engage with their financial advisors during this time.

They'll assess the company's worth. They'll select a price they're prepared to pay for this firm and then make an approach to the target firm with their experts.

Now, this can be done by advisors. This may sometimes be accomplished through personal connections. However, there must first be a discussion between the two of them.

If the acquisition is a public offering, the acquiring firm will publish a business press offer to shareholders for their stock to the business press.

That may or may not involve a discussion and a meeting with the target company's board, depending on the hostile or friendly nature of the transaction in a private deal.

Several of them are bound by certain parts of this letter of intent. The majority of them are non-binding or subject to the sale and purchase agreement.

They'll also be subjected to due diligence, which is when a buyer's company goes in and meticulously checks all of the legal and accounting documents as well as every detail of the target firm to ensure there are no skeletons in the closet.

Then, of course, the letter of intent is subject to discussion. The acquiring company does not have to accept it.

Then, of course, if it's a private agreement, the parties must protect one another's secrets.

If the approach is accepted, you'll still have to wait for a response from the target organization. As well as accept the offer that seldom happens.

It's also more likely that they'll reject it or negotiate the terms, price, type of consideration, timetable, and so on.

They'll want to have a discussion and negotiation and try to improve the agreement.

From their standpoint, the buyer may not be well-liked at all, and they could look for alternative bids from other purchasers.

This is especially the case for a public company, when it is deemed to be put in play and seen publicly as a takeover target.

All of this speculation and guesswork arises, as well as the prospect of management coming up with a solid explanation for why they've declined it.

This scenario might also include approaching private equity firms to take over the company rather than the buyer who is making the approach.

If the agreement is significant enough, it will have regulatory consequences.

There will be regulators, the SEC, and the FTC. The authorities include the stock exchange, who will get involved especially in cases of monopolies or regulated, regulated businesses where the regulator will have a say on the terms of the agreement.

If you're thinking about doing business with a firm that has a large workforce, there's one more thing to consider: transactions involving huge organizations are subject to regulatory scrutiny and complexity.

If you're making a huge transaction in Europe, you'll also have to obtain the E.U.'s approval.

There are a number of hurdles to overcome, with some transactions taking more than a year to conclude.

However, when you get to the point of closing the deal, you have a situation on your hands where both parties are in agreement, all necessary due diligence has been completed, and all relevant paperwork has been obtained.

Let me give you an example: I've done a lot of these transactions, and when it comes time to close the meeting, there's a huge table stacked with paperwork. And the attorneys usually run the meeting and inform everyone who has to sign what.

However, it is a complicated arrangement, and things must be completed in the correct sequence. If it's a public transaction, you need to finish everything before the markets open so that you can announce the agreement as soon as the markets open, which is usually around seven o'clock in the morning.

So you've done everything necessary to make the transaction happen. In a private agreement, the consideration is paid to selling shareholders.

It's literally a bank transfer that has been authorized, and it goes into the account of the people who own the company, or of those who run a public offering.

In other words, you may receive cash or additional stock in the company that is being acquired. You may also receive paper shares of the acquiring firm in exchange for your existing stake in the target business.

So there you have it. The merger and acquisition procedure is simply a sketch, since there's so much detail to cover. I'll go into further detail about that in later chapters.

Chapter 13: Deal Strategy for Mergers and Acquisitions

I'd like to go through the process of a merger and acquisition transaction with you.

I figured it'd be a good idea to post some LinkedIn profiles or photographs of my experience starting out in Sales and Business Development to give you an indication of my skillset.

I'm currently focusing on the publication side of things.

So I have a lot of hands-on expertise, and this isn't always the case for internet influencers.

So this book that you reading about mergers and acquisitions, is primarily focused on the outcome of closing the deal.

But, if you're new to M&A, I thought it would be beneficial to walk you through the entire M&A transaction procedure.

So you may have a better idea of where the closing bid fits in.

In the first stage, both sides are preparing and I'm not going to try to explain the difference between buyer and seller activities because they're identical operations.

But someone has to make the decision to walk away. That's usually the case.

Then there's some groundwork to be done, such as gathering all of the paperwork and stuff.

They'll have to perform a market search for buyers or targets at some point, and they'll need to select advisors.

They'll almost certainly need to have a board meeting or a shareholders' agreement to execute the transaction.

There will certainly be a lot of uncertainty and ambiguity during this process, so it's ideal to start preparing now. It's also very likely that there won't be any formal shareholder approval until the conclusion of the process, so it's best to do a thorough valuation and SWOT analysis at that time, whether you're buying or selling.

In the second stage, we enter the pre-due diligence phase, in which a teaser is created and an information memorandum is put together by the advisors, often the investment bank to the seller.

There's a lot of buzz about the teaser. You're approaching individuals if you're on the buy-side.

Documents may be missing from the documentation, and a data room will have to be established. And the sooner it's done, the better, because this is a difficult process that requires an index of all the papers in the data room since you can distribute that later before beginning due diligence.

It's the time to do it if the vendor or seller is going to conduct its own guy vendor diligence and produce documents.

Then confidentiality agreements are signed, and the information memorandum is released. So that allows the buyer to look over the company based on the information memorandum, including vendor investigations and due diligence reports.

These funds can be released when the confidentiality agreement is signed, based on a reliance and release letter, which essentially states caveat emptor.

You're not supposed to trust any of these paperwork, but we'll provide them to you for your assistance, ease, and enlightenment.

In phase three, we enter due diligence, which is the initial stage of due diligence and takes place before signing the LOI. The buyer is performing some early due diligence to verify their assumptions about the firm, including Q&A sessions with management and minimal deal negotiation.

And once the letter of intent is signed, it contains the main terms of the agreement and the price being provided.

You then have a more thorough due diligence procedure that includes more formal management meetings and presentations, as well as a lot of around-the-table discussion about the due diligence process and the information being supplied.

This leads to a binding offer and final bid, depending on the processes being used.

If you're working one-on-one, the letter of intent might be enough to get you started on preparing the sale and purchase agreement.

If you have to perform confirmatory research and more questions, you'll reach a conclusion after that.

Then we enter the negotiation and signing phase. And, in terms of the subjective concerns you'll deal with rather than the technical aspects of it, this is essentially what the majority of the book is about.

The contract must be drawn up. The representations and warranties that will be made following this step are also included in the document.

The indemnity, of course, protects the vendor by ensuring that the purchase price and all associated terms and conditions are secure.

If any parallel agreements, shareholder documents, or financial instruments are required, they must be completed simultaneously.

Finally, after you've completed all of the due diligence on the negotiation and completed all of the documentation, you'll have a signing and completion meeting at which time everything will be signed.

You needn't worry that your plans will fall through if you don't have a complete meeting at this time. You may have a signing session, and then you must fulfill numerous requirements before the agreement is finalized.

If that's the case, you'll have to enter the signing phase, which involves preparing and submitting numerous papers, as well as any funds or money that has to be raised.

That's when, while the fundraising will have been completed in preparation, it truly happens.

Then we come to phase five, which is the pre-closing, closing, and post-closing phases. Before the transaction may close, there will most likely be conditions that must be satisfied.

This is where it happens. Then you close, transferring the shares or assets in return for the cash, and then any post-closing modifications that are necessary at least a name change proceed.

Then there may be any post-closing covenants or undertakings, in which the buyers or sellers have agreed to do things after closing.

In a very high-level sense, that is the structure of an M&A transaction.

However, I feel it's possible to see how the various phases operate and why it's critical to get your closing tactics in place as soon as possible so you can negotiate the sale and purchase agreement, do thorough due diligence on behalf of yourself, ensure that your negotiating is done correctly but effectively for yourself, and finally have the transaction closed.

That's all there is to know about Mergers and Acquisitions Deal game plan in the book that you're about to read. That concludes our discussion of M&A Deal game plan.

I'm excited to hear how you like the book after finishing it, and I hope this overview has been useful in assisting you in that endeavor.

Section 3 | How to Value a Business in Corporate Finance: A Crash Course?

Chapter 14: The Business Valuation Crash Course: An Introduction to Company Valuation

This is where I'll start your journey through valuation methods. When I was really starting out in corporate finance, I had a similar experience.

The evaluation of a firm's worth is not an exact science. And it's comparable to coming up with several different, I guess, values and then trying to narrow them down into a range where everyone feels confident.

It's something really tough to wrap your head around. But, as long as you're willing to accept that you'll always have that kind of range, there are numerous techniques for achieving it.

Some are more strict in establishing reasonable valuations of firms.

Now, there are three primary methods for valuing a firm: book value adjusted book value, liquidation value, and profit-and-loss valuation strategies. Profit multiples, price-earnings ratios, sales multiples, and EBITDA multiples are used to assess company performance using the profit-and-loss method.

The principles of discounted cash flow are described in this next section, as well as alternative approaches to calculate cash flow such as cash flow to equity and free cash flow.

There are now two alternative options that I'm not going to discuss, but I want you to be aware of them.

And, of course, there are the value-creation methods like economic value added EVA and then option pricing techniques such as Black-Scholes that become excruciatingly complex.

I'm not sure anybody understands, so how can they have any worth?

Let's think about why we might want to appraise a firm first, though.

It's essential to distinguish between the buyer's and seller's points of view, as well as the value assigned to each. Because they will have distinct criteria and methods, different buyers will have different values for the business depending on what they are now.

The process of determining the highest price at which the seller is willing to sell his firm is known as valuing a company.

He'll be asking questions like, "What is the company worth?"

Don't confuse a firm's value with the amount a buyer may be prepared to pay for it.

So, what are the benefits of having a valuation? A valuation will come in handy in a variety of situations, so let's go through some examples.

It will assist the buyer and the separate party in coming to a view, as well as hopefully about value and eventually an agreement on price, in an M&A transaction.

When assessing listed businesses, it will be beneficial to establish whether they are overvalued or undervalued when compared to their market value, as you would when preparing a company for an IPO on the stock market.

With this information, you'll be able to lay the groundwork for pricing your stock. When it comes to determining the success of a company's financial performance or a senior management team or something under an incentive program, evaluation is crucial.

The valuation process may help you find strategic value drivers in a company.

Finally, if you're attempting to assist management teams and their advisors in carrying out a strategic planning process, it's only natural that the assumptions that go into that process should be evaluated in a valuation.

Remember, there isn't a simple solution to this issue. It depends on your standpoint: buyer or seller.

It all depends on the approach you choose. It also relies heavily on the assumptions you make when using those methods in order to get the answers you'll get from whichever technique you take.

Expect a little of a roller coaster, but it's an important part of corporate finance that you need to be able to demonstrate you can do as part of your job as a corporate finance advisor.

That concludes this introduction. And we'll continue to look at various techniques in the following chapters.

Chapter 15: Valuation of a Firm for Sale

Welcome back to Valuation of a Firm for Sale, where I'll discuss valuation in this Chapter.

Now, because the owner of the company would desire a very high value, and any buyer will attempt to place a low worth on it, valuation is a highly contentious issue.

If you're an adviser, you're caught in the middle because you'll be attempting to establish a value that is objective and help the two parties come together.

I'm going to keep it simple. I'm not going to get into option pricing models. I'll just stick to three easy techniques.

They are also comparable firm comparisons, comp. M&A transactions, and accrual-based cash flow calculations.

Let's start with the first one, which is listed company comparable metrics.

We've already gone through the following steps. Now we're doing a little different approach of looking at similar firms and seeing how they're valued. We'll go over what happens next in the investing process below.

Depending on the company's line of work. You must decide which is most essential. However, you're usually considering profit and loss account multiples and earnings per share multiples.

What you should do is establish a matrix of these so that you can see the averages that result.

This also aids in the smoothing of any market anomalies. Of course, when you look at your Comparables, you must be aware that if there is a genuine outlier, you must investigate and find out why the market values a company so highly or so badly.

You may then use the matrix and the averages of these multiples to valuate a firm, which will show you what sort of range each multiplier has for that valuation.

So the second approach to examine valuation is to look at comparable mergers and acquisitions deals. Deal databases are available to your advisors, but go and look at similar firms that have been sold and attempt to figure out what revenue multiples, earnings multiples, assets multiples, and cash flow multiples they were acquired at.

Examine those firms and apply what you've learned to your own company. What I discovered in the past is that you won't have full financial information on all of these transactions.

If you can get a multiple of profit or revenue, and if you can acquire these distinct data points, and if you have enough of them, you may begin to construct a meaningful range of multiples that you may apply back to the company's mission of attempting to value.

Now, discounted cash flow is a more sophisticated, but also a more objective technique than DCF, because here you build a model of the firm and it must be an integrated profit and loss, cash flow, and balance sheet model so that any changes in one reflect throughout the whole model on your balance sheet must always balance.

But, again, what you're doing is you're taking the company's cash flow for the next five or ten years and I recommend a period of ten years. Then you discount that value to today's dollars to get a present-day value, which gives you a company valuation.

There are quite a few red flags in this approach. The first is your forecasts' assumptions. Second is the discount rate you use, and third is the terminal value you choose.

The valuation of a company in a DCF model is highly reliant on the assumptions made going into it.

As a result, it is still highly subjective.

Another thing I would say is that, when you're comparing market transactions and historic M&A deals, you need to be aware of the current market conditions as well as those that prevailed in the past because, as I'm sure you're aware, the market goes up and down like a yo-yo.

I recall hearing one entrepreneur tell me in the early 2000s that his firm had to be worth 40 times revenues because some person had valued it at that level three years ago, before the dotcom bubble burst.

Of course, the industry had changed significantly, and it was becoming increasingly difficult for him to accept this, because I believe he really wished he'd sold the firm three years ago at those obscenely high levels.

That's all there is to it when it comes to valuation; we're trying to assist you in understanding how you and your advisors will arrive at a valuation range for the business that will be sold.

In this chapter, I'll examine the sale objectives in depth.

If you want to create a successful sales process that will bring the most value to the company you're attempting to sell, there are a few things you should remember.

Chapter 16: Balance Sheet and P&L Statement: The Financial Statements Are the Two Key Sets of Information You'll Need to Know

Hello, and welcome to the chapter on corporate valuation. We'll look at balance sheet and PNL valuation techniques for a firm in this section.

Now, one of the drawbacks of accounting data for a valuation is that you must accept all accounting assumptions and conventions that went into generating the profit and loss statement and, in turn, the cash flow statement as shown in a set of accounts.

These are not intended for company valuations. These are meant to assist you in understanding the company's financial health over a 12-month period, as seen in the profit and loss account and balance sheet.

It's a moment in time, as of the balance sheet date. And of course, accruals are involved. This includes book value, depreciation rates, and a variety of rational criteria to achieve the purpose for which it was created.

But it's not about the price. And because of this, it's critical that you consider this before you start utilizing these figures, which have been meticulously calculated by accountants to value a business.

So, with that in mind, let's look at some of these approaches.

When you're considering balance sheet techniques and valuation, you're basically trying to figure out how much the firm's assets are worth.

Net assets, in accounting terms, are the overall value of a firm's assets minus its liabilities. The difference between assets and liabilities is defined a "Net Worth".

It should be positive. In this method, we look at both net asset value (NAV) and book value.

Adjusted book value tries to compensate for some of the risks that may result from accounting standards such as those I've described, including adjusting or updating the value of land and property, taking into account the effect of bad debts, or even eliminating the overstatement of value caused by factors like obsolete stock.

Now, you can get a different viewpoint on a company's worth by examining the liquidation value, assuming that the assets are sold quickly and modestly to repay the business's liabilities when it closes down.

This is one approach to determine the bottom line of a company.

In conclusion, book value has very little relationship to market value, in my opinion and it's not a good method to evaluate a company.

Let's take a look at some profit and loss account techniques, also known as income statement methods, which use the sales and profits of a firm to arrive at a value for it.

The price-earnings ratio is one of the most common techniques in the public markets. And this compares the market firm's market value to its earnings per share, which displays how highly investors appreciate the business on a per-share basis and offers a really useful, if simple comparative ratio when looking at one or more firms.

You can, of course, reverse this calculation to arrive at a stock price by multiplying the firm's EPS by a certain multiple.

A company's dividend yield is the fraction of a stock price that will be paid out in dividends. This value is calculated by taking cash flow projections and utilizing them to calculate the business's future value.

The dividend is treated as a constant cash stream and is discounted to present value using the same discounting method that we will employ when valuing firms employing discounted cash flow valuation techniques.

A problem for a business is that dividend payments of cash to shareholders might be spent to develop the firm, so you may receive a greater return on your investment.

The growth of lower-paying dividends, on the other hand, would truly outpace that of high-paying dividends.

So it's going to show an inverted result because there's a lot of money coming out and they're being paid in dividends, which you'll then value.

However, you're calculating rates of growth based on assumptions about how much money will be produced in the future, which are incorrect.

So you see the conflict. For years, Microsoft did not pay a dividend due to this same reason.

Let's take a look at some sales multiples, which are a somewhat rudimentary method of valuing a firm and a popular rule of thumb approach to value an industry within certain sectors.

This is an informal way of comparing values for two businesses in the same sector. While it may be used informally to discuss comparable valuations between two firms, it provides no more than a hint of value. If you want to put it another way, a back-of-the-envelope calculation.

Profit multiples; The EBITDA, which is earnings before interest, tax, depreciation and amortization, and the EBIT earnings before interest and tax are two of the most frequent multiples used to value a firm.

The latter EBITDA is particularly beneficial in M&A and private equity deals, since it eliminates interest expenses associated with debt tax, which is obviously something you can shelter and historical goodwill and acquisition depreciation.

When you have depreciation, it's because the fixed assets are being depreciated and goodwill is reduced as a result of an acquisition.

To summarize, these are two purely book entries that have no real cash flow effect.

Now, let's take a look at technology valuations quickly because there has been a long-standing problem when technology firms have been valued excessively highly, often at an early stage.

This is why it's so difficult to value them in traditional ways, particularly if you're expecting stellar growth in the future.

In many instances, pure sales multiples have been required because they are unable to produce profits to value.

So that's it. We've got three views of this. You may value a firm using the balance sheet's components. Profit, income statement, or EBIT earnings before interest and tax are all viable options for analyzing performance using the sales line or earnings, the EBITDA.

You can also try sales multiples for technology firms if your earnings are zero, and you may have to do so.

But be cautious because you're dealing with numbers that are very much influenced by accounting rules and conventions, which were not built or put together for the purpose of company valuing.

That concludes the chapter. We've covered balance sheet and PNL methods of company valuation in this section. I hope you found it interesting,

Chapter 17: Learn the Fundamentals of Corporate Finance in this Crash Course on Company Valuation & Cash flow Methods

I'd now like to discuss company valuation techniques based on cash flow.

One of the most common difficulties with discounted cash flows is that you must first construct your own financial model in order to utilize this technique.

It's critical that your model is an integrative one, since the balance sheet, profit and loss account, and cash flow should all operate in tandem.

The ultimate assessment of this is one that your model isn't circular, and two, that your balance sheet always balances. There's a problem with your model if it doesn't.

This model, however, must be set up with the appropriate inputs in order to produce outputs for your cash flow appraisal and the development of an integrated profit and loss account, balance sheet, and cash flow model is a science in itself.

However, you may calculate the earnings from their company and apply it, but it's not as reliable.

So, let's look at some of the cash flow techniques and the approach itself is probably the one I like most when it comes to company valuation, as long as you've correctly calculated your component parts.

Now, the fundamental idea of the valuation technique is to discount the company's free cash flow projection forward to the present.

This provides you with a present-day worth of the firm. The valuation is very sensitive to certain key assumptions, which is why it's important to understand what your company does and how well it does it before approaching an investment bank for financing or looking for a buyer.

The company's brass always takes a long-term, big picture approach to running the business. The forecast earnings growth into the future, the discount rate you apply to bring the projected cash flow back to today, and the number of years in your forecast are critical factors that you should consider before investing in any energy stock.

The arithmetic used to obtain the terminal value of a company in its closing year is frequently five to ten, and the assumptions you employ when determining the final-year terminal value are critical.

It's also crucial to remember that the cash flow you're evaluating is the only unleveraged, levered cash flow.

That is to say, it does not include the costs of debt financing. This also enables you to assess the company regardless of whether a loan was used.

Now, there are numerous phases to this process, and the first thing you must do is construct an integrated profit and loss statement and cash flow model of the firm.

Now, the model should be able to calculate cash flows for at least ten years, or you risk having a terminal value that is too big a portion of the valuation.

That is one of the drawbacks of short-term methods. You must correctly compute the terminal value in year 10 and then select an appropriate discount rate to reflect back the cash flows to today's dollars.

The most popular approach is discounted cash flow. The weighted average cost of capital for the company is used to compute discount factors.

Now, the logic behind this is known as the capital asset pricing model, and if you want to learn more about it, I recommend that you Google it and look into it.

But for the time being, it's sufficient to assume that the technique computes the discount rate for each equity and debt separately, then combines them into a weighted ratio based on the company's debt and equity financing mix.

The following factors need to be considered when developing a discounted cash flow approach.

Future cash flows will be strongly influenced by the anticipated returns on future investments and the assumed sales growth rate.

The equity portion of the weighted average cap weighted average cost of capital calculation includes a risk-free rate, a market risk premium or better, a company-specific operating risk discount factor and a financial risks discount factor.

When you add it all up, the process is highly contentious. However, your conclusion, the valuation, is extremely sensitive to the premises employed in this step of the calculation.

Finally, one may calculate the breakup value of a company by valuing the sum of the parts of the business and assessing each part independently, but also assuming that each separate business will be sold on a going concern basis.

Let's put all of this information together.

We've gone over a number of the various methods for valuing a firm in this portion of evaluating a company, based on the equity balance sheet, the profit and loss account, and free cash flow from operations.

Of the three options I outlined, I believe that free cash flow is by far and away the best approach to go about it.

So that's all there is to this valuation, and we're done with this chapter. I'm hoping you find the overview of this lesson quite beneficial. I also hope it will assist you in developing your own abilities when it comes to company valuation.

Chapter 18: The Weighted Average Cost of Capital in Corporate Finance: Calculating the WACC - The Corporate Finance Crash Course

In this section, I'd want to discuss calculating the weighted average cost of capital.

Now, this is one of the most crucial abilities you'll need as an investment banker, because discounting a company's value and using discounted cash flow to do so is the proper approach to compute it.

To come up with the proper answer, you must first understand how to combine the discount percentage, which is determined by a company's weighted average cost of capital.

So, let's have a look at it. It's not difficult if you comprehend the component parts of the equation. And essentially, what we're dealing with here is the company's debt-to-equity ratio, because each has its own cost of capital to consider, and you must weigh the components in order to reflect the business's debt.

However, if you make changes to your capital structure in your forecast, you must use a modified weighted average cost of capital to account for the balance of debt equity included in your calculation.

In other words, the company's worth is equal to the sum of its equity value plus the sum of the debt agreement.

If you have equity, cash flow, and debt expense because remember that debt, no matter how hard you try, you will never be able to get rid of the liability. There's an obligation to pay interest on the balance sheet as a result of having the debt there.

The market value of the company is equal to the present-day value of the equity cash flow, and the debt's market value is equal to today's worth of debt payments discounted to today.

Because of this, the weighted average cost of capital is a technique for calculating the blended cost of capital based on a firm's debt as well as its required return on equity.

If you raise the discount factor, it will reduce the company value; if you lower it, it will enhance the value.

Let's examine how to compute the weighted average cost of capital for businesses now. The first step is to figure out what long-term government bond yield should be used in your valuation cash flow calculation.

The second stage is to figure out what the firm's beta is right now, which reflects the company's volatility or systemic risk against the market as a whole.

Step three is to identify the unlevered beta, which has an equity ratio of 100 percent. So, if you know the company's beta and it has a 60-40 financial leverage, you must unleverage that beta to construct the unpasteurized beta.

Then in step four, if you're going to use a different debt-equity ratio in your optimal capital structure, you must adjust the beta to reflect that structure.

Step five is to figure out the market risk premium. This is the historical long-term average difference, also known as the risk-free bond-stock performance spread (or gap).

The risk-free rate is what bonds provide, whereas the market risk premium is the extra market risk incurred when investing in equities. You must first identify what makes up that additional premium before doing your discounted cash flow analysis.

In step six, if necessary, you may add a little cap or liquidity premium for small or illiquid enterprises. Finally, in step seven, you must define the debt equity ratio for the best capital structure in your prediction.

If you change the capital structure in your financing assumptions, be sure that the weighted average cost of capital formula is consistent.

In this part, I'll show you how to create a weighted average cost of capital factor. In the following chapter, I'll provide you with an example of how everything fits together.

Hopefully, by the time you've finished reading these two chapters, you will be able to construct a weighted average cost of capital index in your mind.

Chapter 19: The Weighted Average Cost of Capital Calculation in Corporate Finance - Corporate Finance Crash Course

In this chapter, I'll show you how to do a weighted average cost of capital calculation in practice. Because getting it incorrect is critical,

I'm going to go through each of the components piece by piece, without giving you any difficult formulae that would just confuse you.

The most significant thing is to input the correct amounts in the slots in order for them to operate.

The purpose of this lesson is for students to have a greater sense of how the cost of equity and debt can be quantified. The cost of equity will be our first topic, followed by the cost of debt.

The cost of equity and debt is at the top of the formula, while the cost of debt and equity is at the bottom. The business's unlived equity beta and financial debt equity ratio are both crucial to calculate since they influence earnings growth.

If your investment returns you the same amount of money each day, it's one times one times bracket one plus 50 percent.

The market risk premium is calculated as two points five percent of one and a half. So your score is 1.55. Individual firm market risk premium must also be collected at this stage.

You may also notice that the equity risk premium is seven point seven five percent, as a result of our previous examples.

Consider two more elements at this point: the small cap premium, which measures how well a company's stock performs in comparison to other similar stocks, and the illiquidity premium for the firm, which is whatever it may be.

I've changed the long-term interest rates for two percent and gone over to the government stock's long yield, long bond yield rate for a nation, time period, and company relevant to this industry, from there.

For this example, I've chosen three point three, three point five percent.

The cost of capital, which includes the risk premium and the equity discount, is 13.25 percent. So far, everything has gone perfectly.

The debt is next. Because the firm isn't borrowing money at government rates, it paid a market premium to the three percent risk-free rate we've already seen. Assume that the fee is one point five percent.

So, for the purpose of this example, assume a company's cost of debt is 5% (which may or may not be accurate). However, because interest is deductible, you must compare the corporate tax rate to the statutory rate; in this case, I'll use 30%, which implies that after-tax costs account for 3.5%.

We've added a cost of equity and a cost of debt to our equation. All we have to do now is input the weighted average.

In this example, the debt-equity ratio is 50/50 since you can see from the start.

So the total amount to repay is 6% plus 50% of the debt sum, or 1.75 percent.

EBITDA is a type of financial measure that measures the profit performance of a company. In this case, we're looking at Ebitda, which is earnings before interest, taxes, depreciation and amortization divided by revenue. The Company's weighted average cost of capital (WACC) is 8.3 percent based on the formula above.

I also hope that by showing you how to accomplish this in only a few simple steps, you will be able to repeat it at any time and need.

Calculating the weighted average cost of capital is as simple as that.

Now, those are the fundamental components. I hope you found the chart depicting the weighted average cost of capital useful and will make it easier for you to complete in the future. (Insert Charts and Sheets)

Chapter 20: A More Detailed Look at the Terminal Value

Let's spend a few minutes looking at the terminal value in greater detail.

The terminal value, as we've seen, is a straightforward approach to capture the worth of cash flows that occur beyond the duration of a DCF model.

The terminal value may be calculated in two ways. The perpetual growth approach and the exit multiple technique are the two options.

The second way to track your progress is for it to be more academic.

The exit multiple approach is more commonly employed in the real world and is more often utilized by venture capitalists, huge investment bankers, and other large investors.

The DCF model is supposed to predict the future cash flow of a company over three to five years, but exceptionally it might extend beyond 10 years.

The terminal value, in some instances, may account for a big proportion of the overall valuation. As a result, it's critical to be familiar with both techniques.

The perpetual model assumes that the business will continue to produce cash flow at a sustainable level for the long term.

The formula for the perpetual growth terminal value is TVP = terminal value, FKF is free cash flow to the end, and it's the year one of the terminal value will be the final year of the model.

$$TV = (FCFN \times (1 + G)) / (WACC - G)$$

M&A MADE SIMPLE

Join The M&A Made Simple Discord

●necall.ai

The free cash flow growth rate (G) is the sum of re-investment and new investment, while WACC is the weighted average cost of capital.

The company's growth rate may vary from one position in its lifecycle to the next.

So you may get a rate for the expansion phase, maturity phase, declination period, and so on. It is also feasible to build a multi-stage perpetual growth rate model.

If the exit multiple approach is used, it assumes that a sale has occurred at a multiple of a financial variable if this is considered to have a significant impact on terminal value.

The most prominent measure is EBITDA.

The number of times the event has occurred before is known as prior multiples. The multiple can now be any multiple that seems reasonable to the market and appropriate for the organization.

Of course, comparable transactions may be utilized to provide you assistance.

In practice, you can use both methods to determine the range of values generated between them.

Also, you can use the recurring method to calculate a comparable multiple. And vice versa.

This is a reality check on your model. Is the multiple that stems from the perpetual method out of line with the market, in which case your growth rate may be incorrect?

The calculation of terminal value is critical. You need to know how to do it and what its limitations are, especially because the proportion of the overall value in models that will only last a short time will be so high.

Chapter 21: Corporate Finance Crash Course: Common Valuation Errors

In this chapter, we'll look at the most typical mistakes made while calculating firm valuation, including problems with the weighted average cost of capital and the capital asset pricing model due to errors in discount rates related to the company's riskiness using an incorrect beta for valuing, utilizing an incorrect market risk premium.

Let's begin with mistakes in the discount rate that reflect the company's riskiness.

This may be caused by using the wrong risk-free rate for the calculation. When the historical average risk free rate is taken rather than one with a time profile that matches the cash flows, this might be the case.

It's also a terrible idea to use a short-term government rate rather than a longer term one.

Mistakes can also be made while calculating the real risk free rate.

It is easy to use a historical industry, beta, or an average beta for similar firms when calculating the beta, even if the outcomes seem out of line with the valuations of comparable businesses.

When utilizing the firm's historical beta, you run the danger of making the same mistake as before.

You should not assume that the beta calculated from past data fully accounts for the country risk of the firm you are valuing, which might result in either an over or undervaluation.

A frequent error is to use the incorrect formula in your calculation, which can result in overleveraging of your beta.

Do not make the mistake of assuming that a beta for a company in an emerging market is the same as one calculated on a major developed market index.

The goal is to not confound apples and pears. It's also a typical blunder when doing an appraisal in the context of an acquisition to use the company's beta as a comparison, resulting in the target being acquired in order to estimate it.

It's a myth that the market risk premium and the equity premium are the same thing. They're two separate things, and they should not be used synonymously.

Equally, you should not assume that the market risk premium is zero. The weighted average cost of capital incorrectly calculated by ACSI; This may begin with anything as minor as an incorrect definition of the weighted average cost of capital, so double-check that you have a clear understanding of what you're working with before beginning.

Make sure the debt to equity ratio you use is appropriate for the company's balance sheet balances.

As a reality check, your weighted average cost of capital should not be lower than the risk free rate.

Each business in a diversified firm should be calculated separately in the WACOC.

You may also go wrong if the value of your company's debt is reduced, even if the debts market value differs from the book value of your company's debt.

This will distort your debt equity ratio calculation. Do not arrive at a WACOC by making assumptions about the capital structure and subtracting out the company's outstanding book value of debt from the business's enterprise value.

Let's have a look at some of the most common risk assumptions. The most evident blunder is to ignore country risk entirely.

Do not assume that a substantial deterioration in an emerging market's performance will automatically result in an increase in the beta to leading developed market indices.

An agreement with a government agency, on the other hand, does not eliminate country risk by implying underwriting of the prospects of the firm with whom the agreement has been made.

Do not believe that the beta is included in the calculation. There's country risk, a liquidity premium, and a small-cap premium to consider as well.

Don't assume that beta's given to you include country risk, illiquidity, premium, or Small Cap premium; these risks should only be included when it is appropriate.

It is possible that the additional premiums are not automatically relevant, and you should analyze each situation on a case-by-case basis.

A small cap premium, in addition, is not the same for all firms, and each one should be assessed separately.

Let's recap, we've looked at some of the most typical mistakes made while determining company valuations, including using the wrong data for the valuation, utilizing an incorrect market risk premium, calculating weighted average cost of capital incorrectly, and making incorrect country risk assumptions when computing country risk.

I hope you gained a better understanding of the intricacies and traps that may arise when computing and attempting to value a very complicated firm.

Section 4 | Pre Planning

Chapter 22: How to Get the Most Value When You Sell Your Company

Welcome to Selling a Business, where we'll teach you how to make the most of your company's value when it goes up for sale.

The goal of this book is to assist you in maximizing the value of your firm when it comes time to sell it.

I don't make things up when I tell you that I've looked at businesses from all perspectives. On the buy side, I've acted. On the sell side, I've done business in every currency and type of transaction imaginable. Domestic transactions have been my specialty. Cross-border deals are where it's at for me!

I've worked with both trade and financial investors, among other things.

It's my pleasure to be here to attempt to assist you comprehend some of the context information.

This is stuff that most people don't know. I'm not going to educate you on the deal process.

I'm not going to explain what a due diligence list is. I'll attempt to give you the lowdown on the background facts.

You need that to avoid making mistakes and falling into novice traps, which will eventually cost you a lot of money and prevent you from reaching your full potential.

The fourth is the most important, and it's broken down into four categories.

I'm going to discuss some of the activities you should accomplish as soon as possible throughout the early planning process.

It's also crucial that you get these exactly correct before beginning to promote your business.

There are a few crucial things to remember about the presale planning stage.

And that's what's going to happen over the next few minutes. Then I'm going to explain how you can prepare for the sales process, followed by the last phase of marketing the process.

This is not a step-by-step guide on how to sell your company.

This is meant to assist you in focusing on what you must accomplish during that process so that you may get the most out of your business.

So I'm hoping you'll find this information to be quite helpful.

I'm thrilled you're here, and I'm very eager to work through this book with you in order to help you get the most out of your company.

So let's get this party started and look at the chapter where we'll go through transaction execution.

Chapter 23: Understanding the Sale Procedure

I just wanted to spend a few minutes going over the sales process so you may have an idea of what's involved if you haven't done it before.

Now, the first stage in selling your firm is all about planning and preparation.

It's also critical that you go through a full phase of preparing your firm for sale, because potential buyers will catch you if you don't want to sell.

In addition, you'll discover that the whole process is considerably more stressful and disruptive to your company. As a result, you'll need to examine the many elements of your business' operations, finance, and management concerns and structure.

But, as well, you must keep an eye on all of the potential dangers.

I've been doing this for a while and I know it doesn't take too long to clean up the mess. Imagine if someone were to come in and do a comprehensive examination of your company. You don't want them to find many things that are wrong.

That's precisely what will happen when potential customers enter the due diligence phase.

So it's preferable to get everything cleaned and organized before you start rather than attempting to conceal yourself while trying to tidy up the mess in the background.

Let's get started with the paperwork that will be needed in this instance.

The confidential information memorandum, which your advisors will assist you to create, is the major documentation you'll need.

This is basically the book. It might be 50 or 60 pages long, laying out the fundamental elements of what clients in your company buy.

And there's a structure to this, which isn't the time to go through the detailed structure, but it is the book on which they'll learn a lot about your company.

It also aids them in determining whether or not they should make an offer for the firm if they don't want to support it during the marketing stage and on a no names basis.

There's also a one-page teaser, which is a very high-level overview of the whole Firm. In many cases, it's the executive summary from the investment memorandum that serves in this capacity.

This is distributed out on a no-names basis to assist with early contact with potential customers.

I frequently get questions from investors like: "I'm interested in investing. What is the company worth?" I use something I often call an "investor script", which is kind of like a six-point checklist of the things.

Now, you can't be too hard-line about it since different clients will have varying justifications.

So you need to modify that in order to really address the rationale for the buyer you're conversing with, in order for them to understand why they should be willing to pay a strategic premium for this firm.

Then, there's the management presentation, which is the one you ask to give when meeting prospective buyers.

This should be done meticulously and effectively, since it gives a lot of confidence to potential purchasers in the whole process and management team of the firm.

Your financial experts will now go through a procedure to find possible purchasers for your firm.

Here's where things get complicated. Now, you're looking at a much bigger range of individuals.

People from outside of the United States are frequently the finest strategic buyers, and they may be in the United States or Japan or India.

They may be located almost anywhere in the world as long as there is a compelling need and they are trustworthy.

This might be the case if you're in a different market and wish to grow your business.

They may be interested in some of the expertise or technology that your firm has developed.

There could possibly be new entrants in a particular market. This may be a firm with operations in the same nation entering a distinct product market, or it might be someone from another country establishing a successful business in the same location.

They could be financial investors who specialize in your field and would want to include your firm to their portfolio.

They will then frequently wish to maintain many of your existing managers.

So it's management buyout. Management buy in is when you hire outside managers. That isn't something I would encourage. It is considerably better to have a management buyout instead of hiring external managers.

Then, finally, the most important thing to remember when looking for these investors is that you're looking for people who are ready to pay a strategic premium and who recognize your company because they can see how it may help them with their existing operations.

Confidentiality is important, especially if we're talking to your rivals, and the first step in keeping it is to conduct all of the talks on a no-names basis.

So we go out and the advisors speak to possible purchasers, but they won't say the name of the firm they're discussing.

The name is not released at the time of purchase. It's only when you have a non-disclosure agreement in place, which protects you and your company's proprietary information, that the name is revealed.

You don't want people to learn that your business is for sale and start spreading rumors about it. This may be commercially devastating.

Now, there will be a lot of management meetings with potential buyers, and you'll need to be prepared for them.

Your advisors will arrange them, but they will also assist you in preparing for them and coaching you how to respond to inquiries.

Because in any procedure, I've seen it happen many times: there's a moment when you're asked a question, and it's just too sensitive for that stage of the process.

But you have to know when to draw a line and say, "Sorry, I'm not going to answer that question until we're much further along in this process," because if you don't do that, then the jury is already prejudiced against your company or whatever it is.

When it comes to managing a deal, you must ensure that the momentum is maintained.

So you want to know what their next actions are. It's also an opportunity for you to learn as much as you can about the individuals who may be interested in buying your firm.

Advisers will now take control of the exit, which is a company sale. A sale of a corporation is really a complicated and thorough process that must be handled very attentively on a daily basis.

They'll create a plan and timetable with important milestones in it. And the goal of that is to try to keep potential buyers moving forward through the procedure.

They'll want to know what offers will be given at a certain point in time, and the thing that won't drag on and never ends.

When that happens, a letter is sent to possible purchasers asking them to submit their bid in a specific way, making it much easier for the firm and advisors to evaluate competing bids.

And this is all a part of the key procedure, which will be carried out for you by your advisers and you will evaluate these bids.

Whatever occurs, it's critical that the momentum be maintained and that the process continue to progress when this is being managed.

It's critical to evaluate and choose the best buyer, since this is when you'll make your final decision. It's a crucial tipping point in the whole process because you'll sit down and analyze the bids that have come in before selecting one, two, or three buyers as preferred bidders to work with and negotiate with.

Now, you'll obviously need to evaluate them as a group and figure out how much they're offering and how they plan to pay for it.

So, in order to assess the offer, you must first understand how they plan to integrate your business with theirs and their potential to pay a strategic premium.

It will be crucial to you. It should be critical for you to comprehend their long-term goals for your present management and staff members.

As you know, every project has its own timetable. And you'll want to know what their schedule is like. If I may spell time correctly, that would be helpful as well. Then, of course, you'd want to know about the due diligence they intend to accomplish themselves; however, your advisors will have a due diligence pack data room prepared to manage that process.

It's always a good idea to inquire of the potential purchasers if there's anything particular or unusual that they want addressed in your offer because you didn't do your due diligence procedure.

When it comes to final and best offers with your short list of preferred purchasers, you must keep the competitive tension going.

Don't forget, if you're short on buyers, it's possible that you only have one. You may always haggle with them against the do nothing option, which means that if they make a good offer later, you won't necessarily do a transaction.

It's critical that you and your advisors agree on what your negotiating position will be and how you'll use it in the meeting.

Don't be hasty. And then, at the end of this, you choose your preferred buyer from a long list of potential purchasers.

However, if you sign the contract with one firm now, when you get into due diligence, you'll have a lot of attorneys on your tail.

You'll have the accountants working on the company, auditing all of the figures and haggling over working capital.

It's important to be prepared for any one of these, since if you get it wrong, it can be extremely costly. And there may well be groups of subject-matter experts producing market reports or environmental reports or whatever else you'll have to deal with.

Your advisors will deal with it, but be prepared for it.

Then, of course, in parallel with all this, the sales and purchase agreement, which is the essential document for the ultimate site at the end of the sales process, will be prepared and bargained.

It will take time and effort to prepare that document correctly.

It's critical that you spend time on it, and that you have a strong group of attorneys working for you throughout the process of closing.

Don't forget that a contract isn't final until it's signed. It isn't signed until the ink is dry, so keep your options open and be prepared for the other side to try to salami slice you during this whole last process.

You must be prepared for it and prepared resist.

Another way to prevent your negotiating position from being eroded is to ensure you've got alternatives for this particular buyer as soon as they believe they're the only game in town, since then your negotiating position will be severely weakened.

So I hope that helps you to comprehend something of the sales process. It's a difficult situation.

I've done this many times, and I'm positive you have a fantastic crew of advisors around you who can walk you through the process.

However, if you grasp it as well, it'll be a lot simpler for your management team and you to go through the process.

Chapter 24: When to Sell a Company - The Importance of Transaction Timeliness

This chapter is about how to get the most out of your business when you decide to sell it.

Now, I'd like to set your expectations for the transaction's timing, so I'll show you a transaction timeline.

Tell you exactly what to expect so that you can prepare.

Now, on the slide, you can see that we have a graph, and on the left-hand side, we're tracking management involvement levels.

On top, we have the calendar in months, while on the bottom we have a timeline with dates.

Let's take a look at the most essential aspects of the timeline to begin with.

This is the first phase of your journey, and it begins with a consultation. During this session, I'll review your current situation and provide you with a number of options for how we may proceed together. Then there's a period of time known as preparation, which lasts until the project reaches its second stage (marketing). The completion stage follows after.

At the outset of the timeline, which is assumed to begin in December so that you're ready to roll in January, you must first get to know your advisor and agree on the appointment terms and sign the engagement letter.

Then it's time to get started, and in January you're into the planning phase. The adviser will need to work closely with you, your management team, and any other key personnel in your company in order to develop the information memorandum, which will be the core sales document for your business.

At the same time, while the consultant is occupied, he will be consulting you and assembling a possible buyer list; once these two steps have been completed, the adviser will begin marketing your company immediately.

What do you typically do when you send a salesperson to introduce your goods or services? In the past, I used this technique with my clients.

They can get the information memorandum if they signed a non-disclosure agreement and indicated a desire for additional information.

If they appreciate the information document, they may be more inclined to have early talks with management.

Now, without getting into too much depth, an adviser may want to see indicative offers before he gives management meetings.

In general, in the first three months of your marketing campaign, you can anticipate a lot of discussions with prospective advisers, potential meetings, and then at some point you'll want to receive or the advisor will want to receive indicative offers from these purchasers once they've been evaluated.

Then, if you decide to proceed with the transaction, you may have a second round for "best and final offers" with the appropriate amount of individuals.

That may also take up more management time, and they may need to meet with you again and do further research.

If you do nothing else, at least then set the date on your calendar for when you will be able to identify the individual or entity with whom you want to conduct the transaction.

At this stage, the heads of agreement are exchanged, and then the due diligence on the company and contract work begin.

A buyer will be performing diligence.

Not only will both sets of lawyers be working on the sale and purchase contract, but they'll also be poring over numerous versions of the document in order to get it ready.

Then, finally, in between June and July, the agreement may be completed.

So, as you can see, the process is rather complicated.

I'd also like to thank Grant Thornton for the graph, since I couldn't improve it any more.

So I've taken the liberty of using it, and I fully recognize the composition. So they'll have the money in a few days.

So, to maximize the value of your business, you need to know ahead of time what sort of procedure you'll be subjected to and how difficult it will be and have a sense for how long this process might last if you want to get the most out of your business.

Now, in the following chapter, I'll look at how to prepare for the sale of your company.

Chapter 25: Planning for the Sale of a Business

In this selling a business chapter, I'll discuss with you as the company's owner about how to go about preparing for the sale of your firm.

And I want you to picture yourself seated at the table with your board of directors, and you're the owner of the company.

If you were to list your holdings, it might be that the directors have a few shares and you want to sell your firm.

And that is the sort of agenda you'll need to lay out in order to describe and discuss why you've chosen to take this step with them.

Imagine you're sitting around the board, and the first thing you need to do is conduct a quick assessment of the firm.

So you must have a solid grasp of your company's activities, divisions, procedures, and profitability to determine what it does well.

You'll need to have all of this information at your fingertips because, let me remind you, you'll need to talk about it with your advisors as well.

As a result, staying on top of everything is critical.

So you'll need to go through each of your reports and each section of your company, in detail.

The most recent statistics, latest business plans, most up-to-date forecasts, and a solid understanding of what's going on are all things your advisor will want to talk about with you.

And, of course, the first thing you should ask yourself is whether or not your enterprise is sellable.

Let me give you an example.

If the company is totally reliant on you and your contacts, as in you're just a one-man band with a couple of TVs, you most likely don't have a business; rather, you have lifestyle revenue.

You'll also need to make sure that if you're going to sell the business, it can operate without you or the buyer will demand that you stay actively involved for a certain length of time while the transition is completed.

Is it a valuable business asset? Can profit be made off of it? Is there anything you can do to improve your profitability or defend yourself in court if things go wrong? You know, so is it a company asset that someone would want to purchase?

The question now becomes: why are you selling?

So, why are you looking to sell your company? What is your end goal when it comes to selling the firm?

Is it because you want to take a lot of money off the table? Is it because you wish to live a different lifestyle?

Maybe this is just one of numerous enterprises that you run and feel you can take no further than where you've already been able to get it.

Maybe you've been thinking about moving out for some time and this is a good moment to do so.

Perhaps your market has gotten extremely competitive. And you may see that this represents a fantastic opportunity to sell to a smart buyer who will truly benefit from the purchase and pay a premium price for it.

However, you must have a clear purpose for wanting to sell your firm.

You'll also need to be able to explain it to your management and advisors.

The final step is to examine the firm's financial performance and future expectations over the previous three years.

I urge that you have a detailed month-by-month forecast for the next 12 months, and maybe a quarterly forecast afterward.

However, don't forget that you'll be promoting this firm on the basis of its prior success, but on the promise of future growth and profit that the new owner will be able to take advantage of when he or she purchases it.

You really have to be diligent about your numbers.

It's also ineffective to expect the financial counselor to do so since if you don't comprehend and can defend the figures in depth, you won't instill any confidence in a buyer.

The management team is the next item to consider. It's critical that you have a strong management team, both at the board and secondary levels.

You must ensure that all of your succession problems have been addressed. And, most importantly, if you are the CEO and are exiting the firm, make sure there is someone in place to run it who has already been identified within your management team.

But now, it's conceivable that when the new buyer arrives, he'll put his own guy in charge.

That's one point. He'll most likely have your CEO reporting to someone in his company.

But, whether you're pitching your business to a potential buyer or not, you'll need to make sure that you've got an excellent management team in place.

In the following section, I'll discuss how we arrive at a value for our company. We'll get there in a moment.

Even though you're planning to sell your company, it's still important to have a firm understanding of what you expect the value of your business to be. I also suggest that this is not a hard and fast number.

It's most likely going to be a scale. I've heard many times that a business owner has turned to me and said, "My company is worth $10 million or £10 million."

So I'm thinking, OK, well, that's great. What reasoning have you based your claims on?

He explained, though, that he wanted to retire with this money. And when I look at the company as a whole, I have to go back and revisit even the awful news: that I'm sorry.

I'd estimate that your firm is only worth between four and five million pounds (about $5 million) or four and five million dollars.

As a result, your knowledge of valuation and expectations must be realistic since if you have a target figure but the company behind it doesn't actually connect to the right numbers, it's no good.

It's crucial to be specific about how you estimate assets. Finally, the time of the sale is important.

So, now that you're aware of the fact that it will take six to seven months to complete this procedure, which I showed in the first session.

So you should consider when you'll begin it. You also need to realize that it will take up a significant amount of your and your management's time, which may be very inconvenient for the company if you haven't prepared for it.

So, these are some of the most important issues to consider when preparing the sale of your firm.

In the next chapter, I'll talk to you about valuation because this is a crucial distinction.

It's critical that you, your management team, and your advisors are all on the same page before beginning the marketing campaign for this firm.

Chapter 26: Selling a Business - Objectives During the Sale

Welcome back to My Business for sale.

In this section, I'd want to discuss a sales goal, because it's critical that the vendor, board, and advisors all have the same goals for these issues.

The first issue to consider is what the vendors' goal for the transaction is.

So, why is he or she or the group of shareholders selling the firm and what do they hope to achieve?

You must also question them on this because if you don't do so, you won't be able to determine whether or not your sales process has been effective as an adviser or a board.

So, first and foremost, you must know what kind of price target is expected?

This should be represented as a range provided by the vendor or the vendors for the company.

It's also worth if you're advising the firm or are on the board of directors doing some research before you ask them this question, presumably at a meeting so you can have your own viewpoint on what the company is worth since now is when you should challenge any over or under value.

There's nothing worse than completing a procedure and then the vendors turning around and stating, but I've always wanted ten million dollars for this company.

You've also created offers in the $5M to $6M range because this mismanagement of expectations would almost certainly result in vendors walking away and no agreement being reached.

So you need to get this down as soon as possible.

The next thing I'd want to talk about with them, or I would if you were on the board, is how this will affect your staff.

You've been through the motions, and you've arrived at your conclusion. Because don't forget, it's a complex and lengthy process. There will be some sort of disruption to the operation.

It will be a tremendous amount of work for the company's management team.

There's also the matter of if the personnel become aware, and they might at some point in the process, or if they do attempt to keep it quiet. If they find out that the firm is for sale, this may damage their confidence in the company.

If a rival attempts to hire one of your best individuals, they may be more inclined to go if the company is being sold since they will be very concerned about their future.

So, with all this in mind, you need to have a strategy for how you'll communicate with your employees and protect them from the process, how you'll protect them if they learn about it, how you'll manage confidentiality, and so on. So there are folks who fall into that situation.

The next point to consider is whether you're seeking for a full sale or a earn-out method.

The vendor now values the company at a certain price, or gives them a lump sum in exchange for it. And walk he or she walks away, and the earn out is paid. This has to be planned meticulously.

However, in principle, at the end out, then the owner or vendor is involved in the firm over time and part of their payment for the company is paid in tranches as long as certain objectives are met.

So, what do they want? What sort of bargain are they searching for you to create for them?

From the perspective of a buyer, the fact that the owner, the vendor leaves quickly is an increased risk transaction.

If they continue to be engaged in the firm, because once you're inside the business and dealing with them, you'll discover any issues, but you'll have a period of time where they're involved in the company where if they don't fulfill their forecasts, you won't have to pay them as much money for the firm.

As a result, it's a safer transaction for the buyer.

So, first and foremost, you must know what kind of bargain we're discussing. The next item to address is how will the consideration be delivered?

This is a straightforward either/or option. It will be in cash, or it will be in the form of paper, which may be a low note. It might be equity shares, for example.

What kind of offer are they seeking?

Normally, sellers want cash for their business, but when a huge transaction like this technology trade is being considered, you'll discover that the majority of the consideration is in cash and only a tiny amount is in shares.

This was particularly significant in the dot com era. And, of course, when this occurred during that time, a lot of people were paid handsomely and highly rated stock certificates were issued.

When the bubble burst, those shares were worth a huge amount of money—or, in many cases, were completely worthless.

Today, cash-rich businesses, particularly as Microsoft, Apple, and Google have been paying out transactions in cash.

From the vendors' standpoint, it's a lot of money to receive because they're receiving, you know, these very large payouts in cash.

The third and last issue I'd wish to address is whether there will be a handover period or if vendors will depart immediately.

In addition, it's quite common for them to have a short handover time so that you can get help addressing any key concerns.

It depends on how involved the vendor has been in putting the business up for sale if they're willing to give it. This will most likely be a demand from the Buyer.

However, you must first understand what they are willing to do as a vendor to make the transaction simpler for the buyer.

These are some of the sales goals that must be addressed before a marketing campaign is launched.

It's also worth sitting down around the table and discussing these as a board so that everyone is on the same page, recorded, and you can provide your adviser with this information so they know where they stand.

Then, to make your sales process more solid, you should use the method that I'm proposing.

Now we'll move on to the next chapter, where we'll discuss presale planning.

Chapter 27: Selling a Business: Pre-sale preparedness introduction

Welcome back to the Selling a Business chapter series.

In this chapter, I'll talk about presale preparation and, in the subsequent three chapters, I'll go through presell planning in depth.

But I only wanted to foreshadow the subject for you in this chapter. That is certainly significant.

You can't just start a sales process without doing some sort of presell preparations because if you don't, you'll most certainly decrease the price at which you'll be able to sell your business.

The primary goal of the presale preparation is to improve your company's and its attractiveness to a possible buyer.

So, for example, you're reducing costs where appropriate by closing underperforming stores and renegotiating leases with existing store locations. You're doing this by cleaning up all the loose ends, ensuring that all of your documentation is in good order, that there are no outstanding issues of any kind, and that you've done everything possible from a financial standpoint to position your business to get the best possible exit.

You're putting your best foot forward by doing this, and it's the greatest approach to make a first impression.

However, it's like every business has a lot of loose ends that we always intended to finish, but they never quite get completed.

Don't forget that the buyer will perform a lot of research. They'll dispatch their attorneys, accountants, and other consultants to examine all of your corporate records, and they don't want to find any skeletons in the closet.

Now, with all of your documents in a professional order and all of your data properly organized, it's time to go through everything and get rid of any skeletons.

When you do hand over all of your information for due diligence, it will be a quick and easy endeavor since everything will be cleanly sorted out now.

If you do have a problem, you must immediately inform the other party since if an issue is discovered during due diligence or after letters of intent are signed, you'll be certain to invite the other side back to the table and negotiate a better price for the transaction.

Don't forget that the most important thing is that it's truly a "banking without surprises." It's a deal process with no unpleasant surprises.

When you discover a skeleton in the closet, both sides will have questions. It's also crucial to maintain their trust if they begin to ask why we found a skeleton in the cupboard when they've never been there before.

So, as a result, you must go through this preparation stage.

However, keep in mind that it will take time and you should get started as soon as possible if you're thinking of selling your firm because starting now will ensure that the process does not disrupt your business on a daily basis, allowing you to focus on getting this phase correct.

On the other hand, you must be discerning. Not every rabbit hole needs to be pursued. You understand, there will be an 80-20 balance and the prioritization of your issues is crucial.

Deal with the big problems first, then if you have minor concerns, deal with them as a secondary issue or put them on a to-do list while going through the sales process.

Apply common sense to this, because believe me when I say there will be a lot more for you, your management team, and your employees to do.

Don't forget that if you're keeping this procedure secret from your staff, you'll either have to invent a cover story for them.

For example, you'll be required to explain how the business will be sold to investors in a responsible and thorough manner. You may not just omit confidential information without permission!

This is why they're taking the time to check each of the property leases, since it's important for them to know what their obligations are before agreeing on any terms.

This is the pre-sale business's formal introduction.

Now, in the next chapter, I'll discuss some of the legal and administrative concerns you'll need to address while preparing for a presale.

Chapter 28: Selling a Business - Rules and Regulations (Legal and Admin Formalities)

Welcome back to the selling a business series, I just want to remind you that the goal of this series is to assist you in maximizing the value of your company when you sell it.

In this chapter, I'd like to discuss the legal and administrative preparations that are critical before you begin your marketing campaign.

The aim of this is to get all your ducks in a row so that when you go through the due diligence process, you're ready to go and can give all of the documents requested on the long list provided by lawyers, as well as make sure everything is up-to-date and there are no holes.

So the first thing you must do is make sure any outstanding litigation is resolved.

There's usually nothing to be concerned about. However, if you're involved in a lawsuit, this is one of the most significant value killers imaginable because you're leaving an open liability on someone else's shoulders.

If that is the case, they will anticipate the worst-case scenario and demand retention to cover that amount of money.

As a result, it's critical to clean up all of your litigation.

The next step is to make sure that all of your patents and trademarks are registered and up to date.

And you should consider the countries as well, because if you're just operating in the United Kingdom, for example, you may still want to secure worldwide patents to prevent someone from stealing your particularly precious IP in another country.

However, you must show that any IP is protected by patents and trademarks.

If you haven't addressed the problem yet, now is the time to start.

When you start the due diligence process, you must provide a complete set of contracts for all of your key personnel.

So, if you don't have these in place or they're not up to date or they're not standardized, and you have various ones, this is an essential detail that must be addressed.

Now, of course, if you're going to start renegotiating employees' contracts, it will be a difficult conversation.

Ideally, it's all about ensuring that every contract is in its proper place and has been signed and updated.

So, make sure you cross off each one of those.

The second thing to do is check your property and title deeds and leases to ensure that, once you've obtained them, they are correctly signed and accounted for, with no liabilities.

For example, if you find out that you have a provision in your lease requiring you to make good on the property at the conclusion of it, which may cause one to think that the property is in a state of disrepair, which might lead someone to believe, "Well, actually, the property is currently a mess."

I'd want you to concentrate on this area. So go through your property and contracts one more time.

If you have a particularly tough group structure with many different businesses all over the world, you may want to hire your attorneys in to re-organize the corporate entity and make it more straightforward.

If you have dormant firms, there's a chance that they may be held liable for previous debts.

This could be a difficult situation to resolve, but it may be worth shutting down or removing those firms from the group entirely.

In a sales process, if you've got any minorities or collaborative interests, they may be extremely messy and difficult to handle.

If you have any of these, you'll be hit for value.

If you can close them out, as long as it makes business sense to do so or purchase in the minorities, now is the time to do it.

The better everything is made simple and clean, the better.

Consider how you'll be able to manage your finances without having any unpleasant surprises.

Now the environment is a major potential liability concern.

So, to minimize any downside risk in this area, it's well worth having your environmental audit done.

No, I'm not an expert in environmental audits, but I'm confident you'll grasp the concept that if you've polluted the area or there's a lot of waste material around, you need to clean it up and have an audit that confirms no residual liability.

Remember, this is all about minimizing the problems and making everything as clean as feasible in order to give the other side as little cause as possible to renegotiate any terms or include onerous conditions in the sale and purchase agreement.

If you get your act together, you'll be in excellent form for due diligence.

Getting your legal counsel is the most effective approach to do this.

Ask them to conduct a thorough investigation.

As for your company, contact them and instruct them to prepare your due diligence papers now so that you may refer back to them at the sale.

So that you can devote your time to conducting your due diligence effectively.

In the following chapter, I'll look at some of the operational preparations you'll need to make in order to get ready for a sale.

Chapter 29: Selling a Business - Operational Preparedness Undertaking

Welcome back to the world of commercial selling; in this chapter, I'd like to discuss some of the operational preparations you may make to help you get the most out of your company when it's time to sell it.

This first step is your succession planning, which involves determining how you will organize your senior management after the transaction since you may want to sell the company.

If you're talking to your customer as an adviser, you must clarify exactly what the managerial structure will be like if any major shareholders have quit the firm.

But what I want to emphasize is that it's really crucial to sit down and work out this issue now, either with a small group of your senior leadership or however you choose to do it.

You don't have to make any adjustments right now, but you may identify where you have gaps or weaknesses and take steps to address them.

At the second level in your management structure, for example, you must look at and evaluate where there are flaws and gaps so that you may improve it.

When someone from a third-party review agency comes to evaluate the company, you want to be able to show them that you've got a first-class team in command and an outstanding, well-rounded team at the second level.

This will provide them with a lot of optimism that they are making a wise decision by purchasing your company.

Let's take a closer look at revenue growth since that is what you obviously want to demonstrate in this current year: It prepares you nicely for the sales process since it shows yearly growth.

The timing of sales is another one of the things you can examine.

Make sure your contractors are aware of the deadline and that any paperwork, documents, or other items in process have been completed.

Also, be on the lookout for services you're about to begin; these could get delayed even further due to delays with communicating with your clients.

You truly want to get your employees onto it and ensure that you've taken every possible measure to ensure that the revenue is properly recognized.

Consider if you're looking at profitability, pricing and margins, what can you do across your company that will boost profits?

Of course, you may reduce or eliminate any discounts you're offering if you modify your margin structure or adjust it or really scrutinize every discounts you give in that sector to see whether you can hard put them straight to the bottom line.

Now, this is a highly personal account with a laser-like focus on the most important aspects, because it's clear that greater profits at higher margins is the top priority.

Let's take a closer look at operating expenses now, as this is the next portion of your personal account.

There are many different activities you may do to increase EBITDA that will be considered when evaluating a firm.

The first step is to go through and remove any non-essential expenses.

And, of course, it's important to go over your fixed and variable expenses and see where waste might be found.

Another aspect to think about is whether you need to spend the money you're spending on R&D or advertising. Can we reduce it in any way? And one excellent opportunity is to examine your R&D or advertising and ask, well, do we really require to put this much money into it?

Have a comprehensive evaluation of the rest of your cost structure to see what you can do to save it.

There are also some non-business expenses that need to be addressed.

Two of these, in particular, which are major red flags when it comes to having family or relatives on payroll: your wife, your children, or your response.

So make the most of this opportunity to get rid of your family as nicely as possible.

But if you're serious about getting top dollar one, they are taking money out of the company, which will lower your EBITDA.

If you're going to get compensated a multiple of that, then you want to make every effort possible to save that money and return it into the value someone else will pay for your business.

Likewise, if you're putting personal expenditures through the company, stop doing so. It's shortsighted because for every pound you cut your PNL down to, someone will pay you a five pound multiple of EBITDA, which is $1 million divided by 5 years (EBITDA x C)/$5m).

So you must clean up your act and become a lot more disciplined.

So, how are you going to handle expenses right now? Of course, this is only to touch on the surface of things, but what I want to emphasize with you is that it's critical to go through a rigorous cost analysis, go line by line down your Pinal County coast and figure out if you're getting the best deal for your electricity, heating, postage, delivery and shipping or whatever else it may be.

What are your options for lowering expenses and increasing profits?

Because you'll be receiving this back five times over, at the very least if someone pays you EBITDA five times over.

On the financial side, there are a number of things you may do to reduce your costs and increase your revenues.

In the following chapter, I'll discuss what you can do to review the company's assets.

Chapter 30: Selling a Business - Review of the Company Assets

I'd want to talk to you about the asset evaluation and how you may use your company's assets to ensure that you receive the highest possible price when it comes time to sell your firm.

The first thing I'd like to take a look at is your company's fixed assets.

Now, consider that a number of these may have been built up over time. If you've been running your business for a long time, it's definitely worth going over and inspecting what you've got in the business to see what you can do with it and, more importantly, what you can get rid of.

If you have assets that are underutilized, sell them and get money now because when a buyer purchases a firm, you won't get value for them at the time but will afterwards take the money out of the business.

One example of this is when a company purchases another firm and discovers that the former company's building is undervalued, with some extremely valuable art inside.

The buyer received all of the value of the art, and it significantly aided in lowering the cost of purchasing the firm.

This is something that should be done since it may generate a lot of money.

You may choose your own strategy for making an investment. Whether you have experience or not, there are many avenues to explore. Look at the possibilities for investments in your business, specifically assets.

I've just cited one excellent example, artwork that has a non-commercial usage and may be sold right now and will not yield a profit at the point of sale. It might be a good idea to take stock of your current assets and their book value, keeping in mind that values vary.

The most obvious of these is outright property.

If you've owned a company for 20 or 30 years, the freehold property on your records may be worth considerably less than the market value.

You don't want to be caught in the sale process by having an undervalued asset, which someone else can then benefit from.

Finally, if you have business investments, this might be the ideal moment to sell those and then distribute the funds from the company.

At this time, you don't want to have assets in the company that aren't contributing directly to its benefit.

When you look at your stocks now and analyze current assets, there are a few items to consider.

The amount of provisions you've established for your stocks is the first thing to consider. Are they suitable? Are you overprovisioning, provisioned for?

If you have stock levels that you don't require, whether it's because of age or any other reason, clear it out and sell it. Furthermore, if you've got old stock hanging around on the shelves, get rid of it and make some money while tightening up your stock policy.

The next thing to consider is your debtors. Now, I'm sure that one of the things every company has is some old debts that have not been paid and will probably never be paid.

If you're unsure if it's worth it, look at what you'll lose. If that's the case, then write those off and get rid of them because they're just raising questions about the company's financial management.

However, if it isn't ever going to be fulfilled, then get them off the books and don't overstate your liabilities.

By collecting the money from individuals who owe you money sooner, you may improve your debtor days.

This will tighten up the company's working capital and make your business seem a lot more organized since money in a debtor is essentially owed to you.

Really, all you want is for the debtor to be paid and the cash to be in your bank account.

The more you can accomplish this, the sooner your debtor days will be reduced. The more liquidity you put back into your own business, the better.

Of course, if you truly have some terrible debts you know you won't be able to collect and haven't prepared for, this is the time to do so.

Now, of course, the money you make from your business is essential.

I'm about to discuss working capital in a bit, but take a look at your cash situation and see if you're keeping more money than you need.

We'll talk about working capital. You'll be able to tell what the proper level is when performing a working capital analysis. If you have too much cash on hand, consider divesting before entering the sales process because you will eventually end up in an argument with the business's buyer over how much of that money should remain with him without paying you.

Consider paying a pre-dividend dividend to shareholders to bring in extra money where it is needed.

So, let's speak about working capital. This is an extremely disputed topic.

To explain the notion of working capital, let me compare it to an automobile's engine. Working capital is similar to the oil in a car's engine.

This is the business's financial center. The money that allows everything to function and keep moving.

The first thing I strongly encourage you to do is to conduct your own working capital study so that you can figure out what the proper level, in your opinion, of working capital for the company should be.

If you've got too much money in your business, as I just said, divide it up.

Consider the maximum and minimum amount of money you'll require in your business.

That's the sort of range you'll need to be working for, and you should definitely cut off any access you don't require when doing your working capital audit.

You should certainly consider the seasonality of your business.

It's essential to give your business credibility by periodically documenting and summarizing the company's progress. I recommend that you conduct it for a year at least, and likely for 12 months in the past, since working capital is cyclical.

Seasonal businesses, particularly those that are growing throughout the year, will require more working capital.

The monthly timing of your working capital calculation, amusingly enough, makes a significant difference because a lot of expenditures are made at the end of the month, which leads to the amount of functioning capital that's circulating throughout the business changing over time.

It's worth taking a look at because I've seen this happen in several transactions. When the working capital evaluation is calculated from a mid-month date, it turns out to have a considerably higher requirement than the end-of-month working capital review.

Consider how you measure at what point in the month to month, since it will influence your working capital.

Don't forget, this is one of the most contentious topics during negotiations with a buyer and seller since as a seller, you'll want to leave as little working capital in the company as possible, whereas the buyer will strive to obtain as much operating money.

I've also observed commercial equity firms try extremely hard to maintain excessive levels of working capital in the firm since that cash then finances the transaction.

So you need to get your ducks in a row with your financial planners and make sure your accountants comprehend working capital.

I must confess, there are times when some of these tiny provincial accounting firms with whom I'm not naming names, I'm not slagging anybody; they don't understand the significance of working capital in an M&A transaction.

This is especially true for accountants who work with businesses that fall outside the SEC's ambit, and it will be extremely expensive to hire a CPA from an accounting firm with expertise in these areas.

But there are other elements to consider, such as making sure your audit auditors are current. And don't forget that if they don't change them before you reach the stage of the transaction where you have a big debate about working capital since it's always an issue; access working cash is a source of cash for your buyers.

That's all there is to the asset evaluation. So now I'll really wrap things up in the following chapter with regard to the preparation you may do ahead of time for the transaction. In this chapter, I'd want to chat about the information memorandum.

Section 5 | The Process of Selling a Business

Chapter 31: Selling a Business - Memorandum for Information Preparation

In this section, I'd want to discuss the information memorandum with you.

For those of you who are not familiar with this document, it is the selling document that will be created by your adviser or the adviser to the firm.

However, it's a document that the management is heavily involved in producing and must sign off on before it can be disseminated to potential buyers.

Consider this to be your sales shop window for your firm.

It's something you'll want to spend some time on and pay attention to in this letter.

I'd like to provide you with some important pointers when writing this paper, which I'm sure will assist you in producing an even more effective information memorandum.

So, know what I'm talking about, believe me. I've prepared hundreds of these things.

However, I'd want you to create the most successful one so that you may sell your company and receive top dollar for it.

The first and most essential thing to remember is that you want this paper to focus on the strengths of your company.

So, if you had a list of all the things that you believe your company is great at and all of these key strengths, you'll want to make sure that each item on your checklist is mentioned in the information memorandum.

That is a fantastic approach to go about it. Brainstorm all of your positive qualities and make sure they are reflected in the document.

Often, there are portions of a business that are really valuable and intriguing, but which are less apparent.

It may be some obscure IP, a patent, or some unusual market; whatever it is, discover it and release it.

You will be educating potential consumers about your company in a manner that they won't learn from any other source.

Of course, the future is all about expansion, therefore you must ensure that the and I'm thinking now SWOT analysis, opportunities, threats, and that these possibilities for growth are properly highlighted.

That's crucial. It's extremely beneficial to be able to display the many components of your revenue stream and what role they play in the overall success of the company.

Now, it's possible that you'll have to make some one-time adjustments to these figures, but if you can produce a bar graph like this and split it up by profit segments and show their percentage of profits on a comparable basis, this can be quite useful in demonstrating where the true value of your firm resides.

Of course, if you haven't already achieved cost savings or any other kind of synergy, you may want to mention it in the information memorandum so that they understand why your predicted profitability next year will be greater than this year's.

If you're looking for a buyer who's a good fit, gives good value, and has the resources to drive growth, then your best bet is still Enterprise Services. If not, then there are obvious areas of overlap where synergies may be developed.

Now, most of the time it's up to the buyer to find synergies, although you may certainly highlight where costs might be reduced.

If you've discovered them, why not identify them right away?

Another viewpoint is that you're preparing an information memorandum for a certain sort of buyer.

So, for example, you might want to have a version that you distribute to strategic buyers and a separate one for financial purchasers.

The document's emphasis will also differ somewhat.

Now, you don't want to make it too difficult, but if you want to target different kinds of customers later on, whether or not you need a full information memorandum that covers the highlights and buttons that particular group of consumers are most concerned with is something to consider.

The last thing I'd mention about the information memorandum is that avoid hyperbole and keep exaggerated claims out of the document.

It must not be dry. You're unquestionably promoting your company. However, you want to make sure it isn't read like a cheap sales document written in a sloppy manner. It requires careful management and professional writing skills.

But, on the other side of the coin, there's a lot to be learned from this. You'll also notice we highlighted many of your subjects. But you know, what's to be said as a reasonably balanced view while hitting the high points without using much cheers and exuberance that appears unprofessional.

So those are some key pointers for making the most of your information memorandum so that you can get the most out of your company.

In the following chapter, we'll discuss how to pick out the finest buyer for your firm.

Chapter 32: Selling a Business - Choosing the Best Buyers

In this chapter, I'll discuss the need of knowing who the ideal buyer for your company is.

It doesn't matter whether you're a financial advisor, an owner, or a board member now.

You'll have a shared interest in gaining an understanding of the things I want to discuss about finding the best buyer.

There are a number of characteristics I'll mention in this chapter that you can use when assessing individual potential customers and comparing them to these standards.

The first of these is finding a buyer who is willing to pay a premium for your company.

That is a buyer who will receive a long-term benefit and who will be prepared to pay for it, or even pay you not to be acquired by another competitor.

So, if they're going to get an additional advantage from purchasing your business, it's the sort of buy you want coming in and paying a little extra for. And this could be an international buyer who wants market entry.

It's entirely possible that your competition is attempting to consolidate the market. It might be a rival from the same region who wants to expand its product range into yours.

Depending on how you look at it, you may cut this in a variety of ways.

You want to sell your business to someone who can add value to it, no matter what you do.

Now comes the difficult part for financial purchasers: making their case.

In my opinion, however, a corporate buyer does have management experience, is familiar with the market, and is active in it, therefore adding value to the company and being able to pay more.

Someone who can't add value is a drawback.

You can't go wrong by selling to a buyer who is acceptable to your existing management team, but it will make everything much simpler after the transaction has completed.

Having a buyer who shares the same cultural fit, respects your management team, and is likely to keep them on rather than holding sway and making them superfluous is something to think about.

And I've seen enormous fights erupt when the two management sides or cultures are very different.

So, while you're considering things, keep in mind that if you break the contract with your management, will they enthusiastically welcome it?

And the best way to find out is going to meet with them and see how they take it, especially if you're a potential purchaser yourself.

You'll want a buyer who will show respect for you and your business, pay what you think it's worth, give due consideration to closing.

If you have a buyer who is overburdened by overlap, you'll most certainly encounter duplicated efforts and waste.

You understand, and this is something you must avoid if at all possible.

You want to avoid acquiring from people who will cause regulatory difficulties.

And, I'm talking about firms that may be operating in challenging locations, who might be coming in from difficult regions or perhaps companies with a monopoly concern or regulatory difficulty who would make the transaction more difficult to complete.

If you can locate a buyer who doesn't have this problem, then the agreement is much more likely to happen.

Because of this, the complexity is more likely to have a cost impact.

As a result, the buyer who does not have to deal with that complexity may be able to pay you more for your company.

If you can locate a buyer that does not require regulatory or shareholder approval for the transaction, the process will go much more smoothly.

If the buyer does need shareholder approval, it will be subject to these terms, one of which will be shareholder approval.

If they don't receive shareholder approval, you're back to square one. Your deal, on the other hand, could be available in the market.

So, if your buyer does not need to go through this procedure, you should value them more highly.

Now, very frequently if you have a big firm acquiring a tiny firm, they won't meet the thresholds, which means they'll need to go before shareholders.

If the firms are of comparable size, the thresholds may be reached.

Because they're unique in different regulatory areas, I'm not going to try and explain them to you.

However, keep in mind that some transactions, particularly if they are public companies, necessitate these shareholder votes. Some transactions will need these shareholder approvals, and you should prefer a buyer who does not require them to one that does.

Finally, the buyer's demand for less due diligence is unquestionably a plus.

Now, from a buyer's standpoint, he must conduct well-informed diligence.

However, if you've got a buyer for whom the transaction is perhaps little and they're ready to do less research, it's a big tick in the box since making the agreement will be considerably easier.

Never assume that potential customers will not conduct any research.

You'll need to have done your research and gotten rid of all the skeletons and cleaned up after everything I've been talking about in this series of chapters to ensure due diligence goes as smooth as knife through butter.

Those are some of the aspects to look for in a potential buyer, since if you can locate one that satisfies many of those standards, that way you won't have issues finding a buyer willing to pay a premium. In the following chapter, I'll go through a little buyer segmentation to demonstrate how different groups of consumers might be divided and the sorts of criteria you can use.

Chapter 33: Selling a Business - Segmentation of Buyers

Welcome back to Selling a Business, this module is all about how you can increase the value of your firm when it comes time to sell it.

In this chapter, I'd like to go through buyer segmentation in greater depth.

Now, I've divided potential buyers into several categories, and all I want to do is quickly summarize the benefits and drawbacks of each type of buyer.

So, when you're thinking about a certain sort of buyer, you think to yourself, "Okay, so here's what they bring to the table; and here are the disadvantages associated with that sort of buyer."

The first step is to discuss your own competitors.

Now, clearly, there are potential synergies, and it's conceivable to have a fast transaction because they're familiar with the company.

The diligence should be simpler. Because they are well-versed in the field you operate in, they should be able to make things more straightforward for you.

However, there is a major problem with them being simply present to fish for your commercially sensitive and confidential information.

This is something you must be wary of. There are many times when a segment of due diligence material is kept back from these buyers until they're much further into the process, precisely when they've been confirmed to be in the last group of bidders, since there's a danger you'll lose a lot of your competitive advantage if these people get their hands on the information you consider to be confidential.

The next group is businesses in related industries.

This is the point at which a firm enters your market. Let's assume they create Pram's and you make pushchairs, and that their products will overlap with yours.

That may not seem like a good example, but I'm sure you understand what I'm talking about.

They will frequently be willing to pay a premium in order to obtain your knowledge in order to gain market entry and dominance.

Because they are less familiar with your company, they may be slower.

There's also always the chance that they'll believe, "Well maybe we don't need to do this a little bit strategically shady," and that they will actually pull back at the last minute.

With such buyers, keep this in mind.

And Bombi bimbo. Well, for those who don't know what that stands for, management, buy out, management buy in and a buy in management buyout.

The first is an MBA. It's straightforward, though there are a few wrinkles to appreciate. The situation where the firm's ownership is transferred from the existing management to a new one via an MBA is known as a transition. A change of ownership occurs when a new management team purchases the firm, which is what we're talking about here.

The fourth situation is one in which new individuals are coming in and collaborating with the existing management to acquire it out.

From my experience, embassies are more difficult to execute and are considered greater risk by financial investors.

As a result, they are less likely to embrace them.

They adore management buyouts because they feel they're receiving the inside track with the corporate leadership.

In most scenarios, you'll receive less warranty requests in a transaction like this. They will rely on bank financing.

There are also potential valuation issues linked to the management relationship issue, as well.

Let me explain what I'm talking about. That management team will eventually become a buyer rather than a seller at some point in the transaction.

They will have access to information on all of the skeletons, giving them an inside edge in negotiations with the financial investor, who will be able to make the case for lowering the price.

At the same time, you'll notice a split board, in which you start on the identical side of the table but ultimately end up sitting across from each other and negotiating against each other.

As a result, achieving this from the seller's standpoint may be quite challenging.

It's also, from the buyer's standpoint, a highly desirable position.

Let's look more closely at financial investors who are entering the market and not doing a deal with management, but they will nevertheless take management on.

They can move quickly. They have established processes in place to facilitate transactions, which is excellent.

In many of these transactions, the sellers have the option to leave money on the table.

If the company continues to develop, it may be eligible for a second payout in three or five years, which is like receiving a double bite of the cherry. They've taken their money off the table; they've stopped working and someone else is doing all the work and they'll still get a reward, which is fantastic against these investors.

But, there are no synergies despite the fact that it's possible to come across situations when a financial investor was.

Have a core portfolio company, and he may acquire your firm in order to add it to his own, in which case synergies would apply.

There are also financing risks, as these financial investors must use debt to make their funding arrangements function.

The interest rates charged on the loan will be determined by the banks' lending policies and regulations, as well as current market conditions.

It's also conceivable for your suppliers or clients to vertically integrate and then buy you.

So, if a vendor integrates with your company or a customer opts to return and acquire you, it can be fantastic.

They have a good understanding of the market. They'll undoubtedly share synergy, which is fantastic.

However, there is also the substantial threat of privacy. Because you're trading with individuals, confidentiality is a major concern.

If your audience is seeking for information, you could severely jeopardize your position.

So, when suppliers or clients come knocking as potential purchasers, you must be extremely cautious about how you handle commercially sensitive information.

Now, overseas businesses, firms wanting to enter a foreign market and acquire your company, can be excellent purchasers.

They frequently pay a significant premium for control, which is wonderful.

They may have trouble transacting, however, because they'll be a long, long way away.

That's going to take longer because you'll have to keep on having visits and travel over people.

If you sell to consumers in the United States, they will have different expectations than people located in Canada. Furthermore, depending on where these purchasers originate, they may be cultural obstacles.

I'm not putting down any points. However, the Brits and Americans I've known in the past are united by a common language, yet their corporate cultures are extremely different.

Don't assume that just because they speak English, that they aren't on the same cultural wavelength as you. However, I've always found it to be fantastic doing business with Americans since you know where you are and they tend to be very astute negotiators.

That concludes our examination of the business segmentation.

I hope that this article sheds light on how to deal with various clients in order to earn the most money for your company.

In the next chapter, I'll delve a little deeper into the due diligence process.

Chapter 34: Selling a Business – Brace yourself for Due Diligence

Hello and welcome back to Selling a business, this is the module where I'll help you maximize the value of your firm when you're ready to sell it.

In this chapter, I'd like to go over some more details of the due diligence procedure.

Today, the potential buyer will go through all of your business records to verify exactly what it is that they are purchasing. This is called due diligence, which is a technical term but does not always mean anything to people who aren't familiar with it.

So it's a verification procedure that you must enable them to go through in order to persuade themselves they're going to get what you promised in return for the payment they'll make.

And the first step is to go back and get your auditors notes and papers, as well as any other relevant documents, and to a certain extent, make them available in the data room, which I'll describe in a minute.

Now, when you're conducting a due diligence investigation, make sure you've got everything clear in your mind.

A checklist will be provided to you by your lawyers and accountants.

So, creating that information is very simple.

However, as any procedure will show, the other side will always return with a slew of inquiries, and you must be critical about the questions that are presented to you and prepared to say no.

It's now not to suggest that you won't communicate it further down the road, but if it's particularly commercially sensitive, you may want to refrain from doing so.

Now, where you integrate your due diligence is that you make a complete picture of your company's data.

You may make it available in a data room if that's the case.

Now, in the past and I can recall when firms utilized to do this, you'd typically discover a room that was at the auditors or at the attorneys, but it's usually one or the other, and you give them all of your files and hard copies and monitored access of that room.

Now, of course, it's all gone online, which is fantastic because it allows for more than one potential buyer to go through the information at once and gives you greater control over access and copies.

It's also a much simpler procedure to upload everything into a data room than to make endless quantities of copies in order to complete a data room.

That's what a data room is, in a nutshell.

Consider yourself a possible buyer, and that you're conducting commercial research.

And, as I've said before, you must be extremely cautious about what business confidential information you allow to surface at any point in the process since you'll often get individuals who are competitors or have access to valuable information.

And, of course, you want to make sure that you're not just giving them the information. Following that, they'll go away and claim they aren't interested. We don't want to pursue the transaction or go any further with it.

So I'm stressing the importance of ensuring that commercially sensitive data is safe.

So I'm going to give you three quick points that could assist you. The first is that, when it comes to making a transaction or doing business with another party, be sure to do your due diligence because the circumstances of the deal will determine this.

But particularly if you're being left with a stake or there's an earn out, etc., It's too simple for these scammers to lie about the nature of their business and a variety of other factors, but don't be scared to push them hard for sensitive information in order to ensure that they live up to their claims.

So that's a little bit about due diligence, in the hopes of keeping you on track.

In the following chapter, I'll discuss the deal process in greater detail.

Section 6 | Marketing the Company

Chapter 35: The Deal's Success Depends on This Key Element

The first thing I'd suggest is that you really understand the reasons why the company is being sold.

This must be understood by you, your board, the advisors, and everyone else who has a role in the transaction. Make sure that these reasons are known to all of them.

Because if you comprehend the goal behind the contract, it's a lot easier to grasp how all of its other components fit together.

The second thing I'd want to mention is that you should really plan your company's sale carefully.

I've emphasized many things in this chapter about everything you should be doing before you start marketing your company.

If you get that groundwork prepared early on, you'll avoid a lot of work and difficulty, as well as potentially unfavorable negotiations, which would harm the price of your business.

So, really, do your homework thoroughly.

Now, be realistic about both price and time.

I've spoken about the company's value and how the timeline might be six or seven months.

However, I've also stressed the need to stick to a plan and to put in a lot of hard effort not to let deadlines slip.

So, if you can manage the procedure of completing a transaction in a timely manner while still obtaining a good, fair price, don't restrict your search to obvious options.

Think laterally about where your other purchases might come from, whether it's across geographies or industries or various sorts of financial investors, and so on.

Take some time to consider where these purchasers hang out. You might discover the finest potential buyer with a little bit of research.

Don't settle for the first two or three options that spring to mind.

The key is to pick a price that's fair. Even if you're running the company against the do nothing scenario and genuinely in negotiations with only one participant, it's critical to maintain control of the auction.

But, in a controlled auction, the procedure is most likely to generate competitive tension that will result in customers competing against one another to obtain your company and get you the greatest price possible while you're negotiating.

If you can figure out what the other side's goals are, you'll know what concessions to make and which ones to avoid in the negotiation.

It's all about asking yourself the right questions at the right time. When you're truly aware of what your opponent is thinking, feeling, and wanting, as well as what matters most to them or doesn't matter at all to them, you'll be able to get a good negotiation and a deal that both parties will be satisfied with signing up for.

Last but not least, I'd like to share something about under-promising and over-delivering.

So, if you're asked for more information than what your prospect is likely to expect, for example, it's going to take longer than it does and then deliver it in a shorter time.

That's only a minor example. But if you adhere to that adage all the way through, your chances of achieving a lucrative high-ticket negotiation and sale of your business will be much higher.

So now you have some ideas for establishing a successful closing procedure for the sale of your firm.

I hope you found this series to be quite useful.

I'm going to quickly go through a summary and conclude the next chapter in this section.

Chapter 36: Selling a Business - In the deal process,

I'd like to discuss some of the things you should consider while going through the purchase procedure.

I'm not going to go over the details of how it's done.

At the start of this Section, I outlined a lot of what you need to know.

But I'm going to highlight some matters that I believe are crucial for you to consider throughout the contract negotiation process, and hopefully keep you ahead of the competition.

The first point is to maintain a sense of competitive tension at all times.

Potential purchasers want to feel as if there are other interested parties out there.

Indeed, you do that, and your advisors do the same, even if they are thinly spread.

During the negotiation, don't forget to bring up the option of doing nothing at all. That may always be used as a bargaining chip in your negotiations.

We argue that since we know, if the price isn't right, if the deal isn't right, we'll just keep doing what we've been doing.

So there are methods to generate that tension. The ideal method is to have three or four competing firms vying for your business.

But achieving that isn't always so simple. It's well worth finding out what your ideal customers' goals are and why they're doing the transaction.

If you can get to the bottom of that, it's all about talking with them a lot and hoping they'll let slip some interesting nuggets of information.

If you know what their primary incentive is, you may use it to pressure the price and improve your chances of winning.

However, there are some instances when the buyer may be unclear about what they want.

In those cases, you must ensure that they receive all of the information necessary and that you are as straightforward as possible so that there is as little room for renegotiation after the heads of agreement have been signed.

So the idea is that when you get to the letter of intent stage, where they offer a proposal on the table, which is subject to contract, they have all of the information they need and can't come back to you later and say, "Oh, but you didn't tell us this."

So we'll have to reconsider the pricing. You must consider the most likely type of consideration you will receive.

In the majority of typical situations, money is the most important factor to consider.

You should be ready to accept their ownership. Accepting debt or loan notes from them might make you a subordinated creditor if anything goes wrong with the business, making your chances of getting your money back quite slim.

Think carefully about the forms of consideration you are prepared to pay in order to accept. And, I'd always start by saying, "Cash is king."

At the indicative stage, be very cautious about accepting offers when you understand the terms and conditions for those offers. They will vary considerably, so you must carefully evaluate them to achieve the proper mix.

You're not required to accept any of them, and you may go back and dispute or negotiate each one.

However, you must look at them very carefully and fully comprehend what they are about.

Reps and warranties are two more terms that you'll hear a lot about during the process.

In a nutshell, these are the warranties and representations that a seller gives to a buyer regarding their business. And in the best-case scenario, you want to provide them as soon as possible.

The buyers will want as many of them as feasible. Your attorneys should do an excellent job keeping these under control, given your reliance on them.

I've said it before, and I'll say it again. If you have extra money in your company, you should distribute it.

There are also tax benefits in some jurisdictions, such as when there is a surplus of cash and the purchasers are ready to buy for pound-for-pound. Instead of paying income tax on it, you may pay capital gains tax on it in these locations, which might be less.

There's a little game to be played there, as there is with all things in life. However, before entering into exclusivity, you must ensure that you disclose all price sensitive information.

That is a critical distinction. You don't want to leave any bones in the closet because it will shatter trust.

It's usually a good idea to address the issue first, since it will lead to another round of negotiations on price and will be pushing one direction only: down as you reach the lowest stage.

If you want to include any significant points in the sale and purchase agreement, you should put them in the letter of intent.

Before you enter into exclusivity with a single preferred buyer, you should negotiate them.

So, in order to ensure that your letter of intent is a solid foundation for your attorneys to fill out with all of their legal charges, it must be nothing less than a comprehensive framework.

Don't miss any key material items out of the negotiation and hope they'll be included in the sales and purchase agreement at a later date.

If there's a glimmer of hope in your company's fate during the procedure, release it, put out a press release, and make sure they're informed about it.

If you're after a lengthy contract or something else goes very well in the market, you need to make sure your prospective buyer is aware of it and considers it when making their offer.

So don't be afraid to provide excellent news. And, lastly, I'd suggest deadlines because deal timelines tend to slip, and financial experts must work diligently to keep potential buyers on track in order for them to fulfill the timetable as set out.

This stage might take months or quarters, depending on how hard you work to maintain control of the timetable.

So, there are a few things to keep in mind throughout the deal procedure.

Section 7 | What is the procedure for selling to private equity investors?

Chapter 37: A Guide to Selling Your Firm Under a Buyout Deal

The first part will include six process topics.

There is a lot of information on how to sell a business, including what goes into a management buyout. In addition to that are introductory selling techniques, such as the typical sales process and what is meant by a management buyout. How to value a company, how private equity values it, which is generally somewhat different, and maximizing exit value would be covered.

The second part of this session will focus on financial themes such as EBITDA and EBIT. Then we'll take a brief look at business assets.

We'll go over what it means to be debt-free, cash-free in this lesson.

Then we'll have a talk about normalized working capital.

In the module after, we ask what is meant by the working capital cycle.

Finally, I'd like to talk about negotiating the normal working capital.

Chapter 38: The Sale Procedure

In this chapter, we'll look at the sale process in detail. The typical sale procedure includes six phases: preparation, documentation, marketing, closing, and tracking the letter of intent, the ally, due diligence, and finally closing.

The preparation stage begins prior to beginning the sales process and continues until the owners of the company are ready to sell.

This is when the seller's representatives compile a lengthy list of prospective buyers for the business. This necessitates precise study to identify the many kinds of potential purchasers who could have different strategic motives for wanting to acquire the firm.

A sales document, often referred to as the Information Memorandum or IBM, is prepared.

It should contain enough data to allow a potential buyer to reach a conclusion without revealing any sensitive or confidential information.

A short no names marketing document, which is generally only sent out to a possible buyer after he has signed a confidentiality agreement, may be used if necessary.

During the marketing stage, a company's representatives approach potential customers and share information, followed by a confirmation of interest and then site visits and meetings with advisers and/or management team.

As the conversation progresses, buyers frequently return with more inquiries and it is important to determine which of these questions are addressed at this point or postponed to the due diligence phase.

Following this, the seller expects to receive bids for his business from potential purchasers.

And as these often come with conditions, these often offers have to be understood in detail and negotiated. This negotiation also involves getting the best deal for the seller.

When the buyer and seller have established their mutual preference, the key elements of the transaction are summarized in a letter of intent or frequently known as a heads of terms agreement.

When the buyer has verified their understanding of the deal, they can begin a thorough examination of the company, including all of the confidential and commercially sensitive data that had been withheld until this moment.

Due diligence is the term for this procedure. Expect a typical time frame of around 6 to 8 weeks to materialize.

Throughout the procedure, both parties' legal teams write up all of the required legal documents.

The first one is the sale and purchase agreement, which we'll discuss more in a later module. The negotiation of the normal level of working capital, as well as the deal's closure and money transfers, can all occur once due diligence has been completed.

Minor difficulties may develop in the course of due diligence, and these must be addressed. A further negotiation may be required.

It's essential to get the facts straight from the start about any major concerns or snags in the company.

Chapter 39: What is an MBO - Management Buyout, and how does it work?

In this section, I'd like to explain what an MBO is, which is a management buyout.

This is the situation in which a company's management, who are also its employees, purchases it from the shareholders and uses their own money to do so. In most cases, this cash was provided by a private equity firm combined with bank debt.

In return for their expertise, they typically make a modest contribution to the deal so that they have skin in the game, i.e., some of their own capital at risk.

The partnership is set up in such a manner that the money generates a healthy return while allowing the management team to make many multiples of their initial investment if the deal succeeds.

A normal contract is as follows:

A bank's senior debt is generally a five to seven year term loan. The business's EBITDA is used to calculate the amount of debt. Banks will make loans between two and four times EBITDA, depending on market conditions.

Banks currently lend at the lower end of this range, if they lend at all. These loans are unsecured or partially secured against the company's assets.

This is called leverage, and it's one of the reasons these corporate acquisitions are sometimes known as leveraged buyouts.

The private equity firm then contributes the next level of cash. They typically invest 90 percent or more of their funds in the form of preferred debt so that they can rank immediately behind banks.

In addition, a residual debt is one which you can pay off over time. A residual obligation will have an interest rate that may be paid yearly or accumulated up.

The interest rate that they are looking for is part of the return they hope to achieve

The remaining investment money from the private equity fund is invested in common shares and is handled by the management team.

The management team's stake in the firm may be a mix of shares they already own and rollover into the transaction or purchase for cash.

There is often another component available to the management team called Sweat Equity.

The proportion of the equity split is determined by the investors and the specific deal circumstances, most private equity firms demand a majority of the ordinary shares, which is more than 50% in most cases.

The sweat equity pot can be up to 20 percent of the underlying shares.

Knowing how the deal is structured, debt and equity, is crucial to understanding it.

Who gets what back in?

What determines how the pie is divided when a firm is sold? A corporation's assets are divided between its creditors and stakeholders. The priority of an item or service may also assist you understand how the revenue is shared out once the company has been sold.

The bank debt is generally paid down by the company's earnings over the term of the arrangement, leaving private equity firms and management teams to split the proceeds of sale.

The preferred debt is paid off first, followed by the remainder of the money. The majority of the assets are distributed to common stockholders in proportion to their equity stakes.

Chapter 40: How to Value a Business in an MBO

Let's assume that you've decided to sell your business. When it comes to valuing a firm, there's no need for fancy MBA jargon or academic theories; all you need is the seller's asking price and the buyer's bid.

Stock market valuations are utilized to calculate company values and acquisition premiums.

But this is not the situation for private firms.

It's also crucial to keep in mind that different buyers would give a company varying values based on their own meanings for the company, what they want to do with it after the deal is done, and how it fits into their existing business assets, such as greater revenues, lower expenses, or increased profits from a combined entity.

The information in the reports is, therefore, relatively meaningless.

Advisers may examine transactions completed by potential buyers or companies in a similar sector at the same stage in the cycle.

The elements in such an analysis are such that either side may make a case for their stance, particularly when dealing with abnormal partnerships, whether large or small.

In a nutshell, the seller will present his high-value argument and generally be willing to accept a price lower than this, however most likely with a fixed minimum.

If you're a seller, it's critical to keep this in mind. A buyer will provide a low price scenario, especially for his first offer, then increase the amount if he has opportunities to do so while attempting to discover the seller's minimum asking price.

The buyer will also have a maximum above which he will not or may not be able to go from the seller's standpoint, and more buyers can be utilized against one another to create an auction tension.

When opposing a buyer's maximum price and the seller's minimum price, there must be an overlap between the two.

Advisers' duties in the preceding module are to assist their client's bridge the gap until an agreement is reached in the next module.

We'll look at how private equity companies value businesses to help you understand why they do it the way that they do.

Chapter 41: How Do Private Equity Firm Value a Company?

How do private equity firms value a company, and how do they assess the worth of a firm when purchasing it? In both cases, there are two distinct trade buyers that price a business based on its acquisition value.

They will first examine EBITDA and the explanation of it provided in the financial models, taking on a stance based on comparable transactions and other market-related data, and establishing the narrow multiple range they wish to pay for the firm.

The exit value is determined by the rate of return they want to achieve.

In summary, most private equity firms aim to double their funding in three years and triple it in five.

An internal rate of return (IRR) of around 30% is expected. But, be cautious with our roles because they are quite time sensitive and cash multiples provide a far safer method for analyzing private equity gains.

A financial model will now be constructed by an analyst and a private equity company, which will enable them to compute deal characteristics, evaluate possibilities, especially on the downside, and confirm their offer price.

The investing research and evaluation of the deal's closing should include a review of the sources and uses of money for the package, as well as how it's being utilized, to ensure that the private equity firm makes its targeted return.

The deal will most likely be financed with some bank debt, and the management team may be putting in equity or a rollover.

In addition, cash or the seller may require debt in the company, such as loan notes to be paid later postponed consideration or a seller earn out.

The capital structure is perhaps the most difficult part of a merger and acquisition to calculate, since it combines all the elements involved in executing the business.

Even if they plan to combine the firm they're buying with an existing portfolio company, private equity firms always evaluate each transaction on its own.

Business synergies, revenue and profit improvement, and cost savings will be more appealing to business buyers.

In this module, we'll look at how a business owner may improve the amount of money they receive from their sale.

Chapter 42: Increasing the Exit Value

In this section, I'd like to discuss increasing the exit value.

Buyers of businesses now focus on a few major factors beyond the issue of strategic fit with their current business, the most important being high margins and high growth scale.

Recurring income, clear difference, and market leadership management quality are all factors that financial buyers consider when purchasing a firm.

Cupboards with skeletons inside are to be avoided, whether they're dealt with or sold.

Sellers who are providing a warranty or representation are allowing matters to be mentioned in the representations and warranties portion.

To avoid this, you must make certain that your agreement with the buyer is signed before you and the client agree to undertake any activity that might jeopardize the deal. It's asking for trouble after the deal closes if you and the customer don't do anything to jeopardize it.

Traders who are motivated by commercial and strategic concerns are the most common.

They are searching for a way to link the offered business with their existing enterprises or businesses in order to build a more powerful and lucrative entity out of the combination.

They may be willing to share some of these advantages with the seller in order to obtain a better deal, but they are unlikely to give all of them.

Financial investors, on the other hand, are more concerned with financial factors. The preceding six items are crucial to them since they are driven by a different set of priorities.

Recurring revenues are crucial to obtaining favorable financing terms from banks.

They're also extremely devoted to the quality of management since this is the team that will execute the company's strategy, which forms the basis of the whole transaction.

In a trade sale, the management team might or may not play a part in a contract with a private equity buyer; as managers, they must be particularly cautious because they face the risk of a conflict of interest.

They each have obligations to the company and investors in their capacity as directors of the firm on the other hand.

When a buyer and seller reach an agreement, any profit earned by the buyers will be shared with them. They will have a financial stake in the transaction after it is completed, making it easy to cross over and act as the buyer rather than the seller.

Executive leaders need to be well-versed in this subject since it is a crucial one for their survival. Managers are susceptible to lawsuits and risk of personal liability if they fail to comply with laws or regulations. This is an issue that management teams must be fully informed about.

Chapter 43: What is EBIT and EBITDA?

So what is EBITDA?

EBITDA is a common private equity metric that most firms use to evaluate the performance of their investments.

EBITDA - Earnings before Interest, Depreciation, and Amortization. It's used to determine a company's net income before interest is accounted for, allowing investors to evaluate a firm's real revenue without regard to the balance sheet structure, regardless of whether the business makes money from cash or pays interest on debt.

Depreciation and amortization are accounting techniques to reduce the useful life of fixed assets or intangible assets on the balance sheet.

Non-cash items like these, in essence, decrease a company's earnings.

This is beneficial to a corporation tax standpoint, but it prevents investors from accurately assessing a firm's performance.

Here's a key tip.

Following a merger or initial public offering, investors will frequently include the pay of directors who are shareholders, especially if they're getting paid far above market rate for their work.

The majority of the time, these directors are replaced by workers who are paid at market rates.

These executives, on the other hand, may include their salaries in their company's overall earnings.

Although in the United Kingdom, it is currently more tax efficient to do this via dividends, which are paid after taxes.

EBIT is a financial metric that is most commonly used to determine how profitable a company is.

This provides the buyer of your business with an income stream from the profits of his company, regardless of how he finances the company's balance sheet.

This is a pre-income stream that the business will not have to pay any taxes to the Inland Revenue.

Understanding these assets is critical, as the EBIT figure is frequently presented on an adjusted basis.

To begin, any one-time expenses such as a bad debt or a significant operational expenditure should be recorded on the balance sheet rather than capitalized.

Adjusted EBIT (income before interest and taxes) is similar to EBITDA in that it is a metric used to determine how successful a firm has been in generating profits. When the existing owner of the business has been drawing a salary or taking benefits, which will not be continued under the new ownership or at least reduced to normal market levels.

The goal of the perspective buyer is to provide a revenue figure that the prospect may use to calculate the company's value.

This module, module seven, is often dominated by the buyer and seller discussing the correct multiple number rather than the level of earnings that concludes this module.

In the following module, we'll have a few words about the company's business assets that are sold during the sale.

Chapter 44: Business Assets

When selling a firm, it's important to think about business assets. The seller must select everything that will be included in the sale.

The most straightforward solution is to require him to include all of the assets necessary to maintain future generations of income and earnings from the business at the level he has forecasted.

All necessary fixed and intangible assets, such as intellectual property, are included in this category.

Changing the basis of ownership, for example, when the seller owns the office but decides to keep the freehold and lease it to the business.

This should be considered in the EBIT adjustments presented in the previous module.

The question of how much money is left in the company and how much oil there is in the engine, if you will, is the subject of our next lesson.

In fact, the financial model modules will focus on discussing standard working capital throughout the rest of the model.

Thank you for participating in this class and I'm looking forward to seeing you again in the next session.

Chapter 45: What does it mean when I say "Debt-Free" or "Cash-Free?"

We'll start by defining the terms "cash-free," and "debt-free," before we get into a thorough discussion of standardized working capital.

This crucial phrase informs the buyer that the firm will be sold without any unsold inventory or outstanding debts.

If either exists after the fact, the purchase price can be increased or lowered pound for pound.

From the buyer's standpoint, he or she will want to know that the firm has adequate financial capital working capital to keep operating.

Working capital, as the name implies, is the business' ability to trade on a daily basis. It can pay people to whom it owes money, such as suppliers and others, while waiting to be paid by those who owe it money.

Customers who acquire a firm with insufficient working capital must put extra money into the company to make up the difference, raising its acquisition cost.

The seller would have boosted his selling price significantly by taking this extra cash out of the firm before selling it.

Chapter 46: What is Normalized Working Capital, and how does it work?

The working capital calculation is used to determine whether any potentially excess cash is available.

This factor reflects the firm's capacity to finance its working capital and pay its creditors while awaiting payment from its creditors, as well as the availability of funds to cover stock or continue working progress.

Working capital is a critical component of cash flow, and each firm's needs are distinct. Negative working capital may be possible in certain circumstances when a business is paid up front for its products or services.

It does not need any working capital since it is funded through its clients' payments, and as a result, the typical, usual working capital calculation is rather easy.

The working capital cycle can be lengthy, little, or seasonal.

It's critical to evaluate working capital on a year-to-year basis, not just the previous three or six months.

Payments received at specific times in a month may be significant, for example, if they are received weekly or monthly.

Looking at the working capital pool on a daily basis instead of monthly, for example, might produce a significant difference in the calculation of normalized working capital.

Chapter 47: The Working Capital Cycle

What is the working capital cycle, and how does one measure it? The working capital cycle measures the amount of time it takes a company to generate cash.

In a nutshell, they're the numbers that make all the difference between your company's success and failure. And, in either case, those figures are critical to get right from both sellers' and purchasers' viewpoints.

If a firm has a lot of stock but hasn't paid its creditors, and yet has been paid by all of its debtors, the seller may try to claim that there is a large quantity of cash on hand that belongs to him and should be paid out of the company before it closes.

If this happens, the purchasers will be in a bad situation since they won't have enough money to pay off bills or to purchase new stock.

If the opposite is true, the firm has paid its creditors and hasn't been paid by its debtors, indicating it has a lot of cash.

When you acquire a firm, it's likely that the company will have little cash.

He collects the debtors, sells the stock, and ends up in a better position than he would be if the correct normalization calculation had been performed.

Chapter 48: Mastering Normalized Working Capital Negotiation

Negotiating the normalized level of working capital.

This is a crucial part of the negotiation and due diligence, and it's critical that your advisors are familiar with it. The winner of this debate has a significant impact on the cash that changes hands at the end of the transaction, as well as other aspects of compensation (such as commissions or closing costs).

Calculating the level of working capital for a company is essential in determining its cash position. The financial condition I will discuss in this lesson includes all of the answers to these questions and more. This money might be worth millions of dollars. In previous modules, I've mentioned some of the difficulties while calculating normalized working capital levels.

Take into consideration the last year. Make a mental note of how many data points you collect on a monthly basis.

To be clear on the significance of these data points in relation to the business payments and receipts cycle, look for any seasonality to ensure that any planned CapEx or OpEx is fully funded.

If this is necessary to maintain the company's EBIT at the anticipated future level, it will be included in the closing balance sheet. The actual amount of working capital and the business on that day will be figured out during closing calculations.

If net cash is lower than anticipated, the seller will have to leave more money in the company.

If the net cash position is higher, he will get a pound for pound bonus.

Remember, this argument starts when the due diligence team enters the company and gets its hands on management financial information.

If the negotiations aren't handled properly, they might wind up at a close, if not immediately resolved, and in some situations ,they may destroy the deal if one party or other believes they're not receiving a fair, honest or accurate representation.

Chapter 49: Buyout Summary

So, there you have it: I hope you enjoyed that part on company sales with a particular focus on management buyouts, which was to walk you through step by step and really give some of the nitty-gritty details.

As a result, you have a better understanding of the foundation and process, as well as some of the most significant elements.

Now, I'll go through the six processes that make up this lesson.

But talk to you through a typical sales approach, then describe to you what an embryo is and how you go about valuing a company under those conditions, the things that are essential to the financial buyer in particular.

We also looked at how private equity valued a firm, as well as how they maximized their exit value.

I go into further detail about the money side of things and expose you to some financial concepts, such as EBITDA and EBIT.

We went through the business assets and how they may contribute to the transaction, as well as the crucial concept of debt-free cash-free transactions.

That naturally led to a discussion about the normal working capital, the working capital cycle, and how to negotiate working capital, since these are important factors for value when it comes to doing deals, particularly with financial buyers.

I hope you found this short vignette useful and gives you a greater understanding of how M&A transactions function, particularly in the context of a private equity takeover.

Section 8: Term Sheets for Beginners: A Guide to Venture Capital Investing

Chapter 50: What is a Term Sheet - Part 1

In this chapter, I'll go over the fundamentals of a term sheet and break it down into two parts because there's a lot to cover.

To begin, I'd like to go through the various components of a term sheet so you know what to anticipate.

A term sheet, in a nutshell, is an outline agreement, a heads of terms, and often a letter of intent that outlines the deal's structure or proposed structure.

This is a road map for the lawyers to check that all of the conditions in the investment agreement are correct.

So you negotiate the major issues, and this should make it simpler for the attorneys to draft the contract.

Last but not least, please remember that this contract is not yet a binding agreement at this point. The confidentiality and exclusivity conditions in it, on the other hand, are typically rather clearly defined.

The intention is that you reach an agreement on your term sheet before putting together a structure, negotiating and signing the investment agreement.

If the series is ongoing, you'll almost certainly need new articles of association.

This is something that you will need the assistance of attorneys with.

It's not something you can accomplish on your own. I'm only describing the framework of the agreement to you. The first item you're likely to notice is most likely the price and the number of shares.

This is all about the company's value, and it's what investors use to make their investment.

Now, the words pre-money and post-money valuation will be used frequently.

The price per share is the valuation of the prize money before the investment is made, which may include warrants and options.

Then, on the basis of that conclusion, investors put their money in and the overall money worth plus the cash they invested equals the post money valuation.

You can now negotiate that the investment is made on a fully diluted basis, which means any outstanding options and warrants are incorporated into the shares owned by existing investors.

You must also pay a fee to the options pool, which will probably be around ten percent.

And that's it for the same reason. So you, as the existing investor, the founders, and entrepreneurs, take a dilution hit on the option pool while they don't.

What is the purpose of their investment, and what type of asset will they invest in?

Let's look at the investor shares. They may invest in a class of shares that are identical to the ones they already own.

So they may be exchanged for common stock or common equity or ordinary shares.

However, they may even have a different class of shares if it's not unusual for them to have a variety of classes of stocks.

Class A, B, C, and A may all refer to completely different classes of shares.

As a result, it's not unusual for this to happen so that investors can have various prices linked with their shares.

Our objective, therefore, is to make sure that the investors don't have any reservations about your firm. They must also keep in mind that future investors will examine what they've done and want to protect themselves against the first series of investors.

So, as you can see, it's not at all easy. So if you can keep your share classes as basic as feasible in the future, it will be a lot easier for you.

Convertibles are another alternative. So in effect, they have debt rights and equity priorities in the event of a liquidation, since convertibles can be converted to regular stock in their circumstances, generally on the occasion of an IPO or a trade sale.

If you have a new class of shares, what are the consequences?

The topic of your thesis paper is important, and it will almost certainly require the re-writing of the articles and topics to watch for.

Is this the liquidation preferences and, in the case of a liquidation event, is it the right to capital?

The sale of a business can also be a beneficial event, such as a trade sale, and the liquidation occurrence, while often considered to be an unpleasant occurrence, may also be seen as a favorable one.

And in fact, if you look at the fine print of these plans, this is exactly what they say. They're saying that if they liquidate only once before, they'll get their money back.

For the other investors, if they're selling their shares and it's a trade sale, that's fine.

However, if there is a genuine issue and an undervaluation exists, this protects investors who get first dibs on the cash.

If you've missed the deadline to remove a liquidation preference, it's simply as though you never had one in the first place.

They get back double their money if it's two times before anyone else gets any cash.

Participating liquidation preferences enable to have a greater voice in the distribution of assets than nonparticipating ones.

That is, if they participate in the program at all, not only will they receive their money back one or two times, but they'll also get paid pro-rata of whatever's left over.

If they are non-participating, they have no more claim to any capital.

The remaining investors get their money back, and then the remaining shareholders divide up the rest of the funds.

As a result, you must be deliberate and consider how you might negotiate it and what is most appropriate for your company..

Essentially, these liquidation preferences are intended to protect the investors from incurring losses.

Investors in these deals are always on the lookout for ways to protect themselves against a decline.

Naturally, if they have a convertible or some other type of equity class that allows them to convert to regular shares on a one-to-one basis, the liquidation preferences would be void.

Let's speak about dividend and distribution rights now, which may have special preferred rates, meaning that they receive a fixed dividend each year.

If this amount is not paid, it may be compounded. As a result, it's possible that it'll grow.

That's why investors enjoy having more shares. They get that sort of additional edge, and they may have voting rates on their stocks boosted as a result.

All of this may be worked out and should be, but you must choose what matters most to you.

Typically, investors seek for board seats at least one per investor per round. And you must exercise caution when balancing your board appropriately.

So you don't wind up with a board that's tied. If there is a syndicate of investors, they might have a seat rate of one but also the right to have an observer at the meeting who can participate yet not vote.

When you're ready to reach out to a VC, your board will most likely need to be rearranged so that you have the proper balance between new investors, existing investors, and founders and entrepreneurs.

This is something that varies from business to business at the moment.

If there are any board fees to be paid, they should be included in the terms agreement and agreed.

Now, most often, investors come in as a minority investor in a series A or B.

They might also have swamping rates, which means they get improved rates in order to effectively manage particular situations where they will want a veto on anything really significant to protect themselves.

Under some conditions, they will have a majority voting position even though they possess a minor equity stake.

And so that is the first part of the module. In part two, I'll go through some of the most important aspects of the term sheet.

Chapter 51: What is a Term Sheet - Part 2

In this section, I'd like to continue our conversation about what a term sheet is and the sorts of things it contains, as well as what they imply.

So we'll start again by looking at some of the successful undertakings that investors will want to be able to enforce.

The investment agreement will generally cover these issues. It might be something discovered during the due diligence that they wish to address right away.

However, if there is anything substantial that they can make clear in the terms sheet, they should. There are also consent issues, which must not be completed without the investor's agreement.

These are generally material corporate actions, such as stock increases or an agreement to sell the firm, which investors will want to have full control over.

You may also notice that they only refer to the general consent rights rather than providing all of them in detail.

If that's the case, you should get your lawyer to explain these terms and see whether anything is amiss between you and your attorney. They'll have to address changes in the capital structure, board makeup, borrowing restrictions, corporate spending control, and key employee hiring.

So, as you can see, there's nothing particularly unusual about any of this.

The next item on their list is what are known as information rates. And this is essentially a statement to the effect that we're investors, but we're shareholders, too.

We want to be able to obtain information on a regular basis, which may, in other situations, only be given to board members.

So they'll want everything from annual accounts, monthly management accounts, maybe a quarterly capitalization table statement, regular access, likely monthly bank statements and updates, and views of the company's business plan.

These are known as customary information costs in the term sheet, and they can be quite costly.

If you're unsure what they imply, contact your attorney and find out if you understand what will be presented.

Let's speak about vesting, because this can be a difficult topic, since investors might want the founders to sign an agreement to re-invest their shares.

This is essentially a motivation to keep the company's founders focused on it and dedicated to it, while also limiting them to just working on it.

The vesting period is how long the founders have to wait before they can sell their shares.

Even though they established the business, they may be compelled to start over and reclaim their shares.

If the creators leave early, their shares can be purchased back for a low price or even turned into worthless pieces, losing their rights in the process.

This is a very delicate situation, and there must be a compelling reason why they want to include it.

Now, the shares may vest on either a cliff basis or simply on a straightforward cliff basis. Essentially, it means that a big portion of them invest at a particular date and then accrue monthly starting from that point forward.

They may also link the vesting mechanism to the attainment of particular goals.

If vesting is a problem, you must carefully consider it.

Let's look at some of the reasons why they may or may not request vesting.

This is less likely to occur if the company is relatively mature.

If the firm is already making money, they may or may not be interested in including the vesting clause.

The investors may not be so generous as to demand that the company be revisited in the same way. They'll look at how much founder investment has been made in the business thus far, because if the founders haven't put any equity in, it's all been sweat equity. They could request this.

If there has already been an investor in the heat, the entrepreneurs may have previously gone through one vesting process and would be hesitant to go through it again for the next set of investors.

Let's speak about leavers who are good and bad, because the aim of this is to state that if you're a terrible leaver and leave under circumstances that may be your contract is breached or you get fired, for example, it allows for your equity position to be transferred away from you so you don't disappear with the entire tranche.

Now, the circumstances under which a manager may withdraw are determined in the investment agreement.

Essentially, being a poor leaver means that you lose your equity position and unvested shares in the case that you leave are worthless.

If, once again, you discover the term sheet includes customary leaver terms, you should get clarification on this and understand exactly what they're suggesting and under what circumstances. You should also talk to your lawyer and advocate about it.

Let's talk about Dilution ratchets now.

These are in place of a down round, which occurs when there is another investment round at a lower valuation to the previous one.

What the investor is attempting to accomplish is that they will try to decrease their dilution by using anti-dilution ratchets, which provide them with additional shares at a minimal price.

This will result in a lower cost per share for the remaining shares, so they won't feel like they're losing money.

Now, there are various methods to measure this. When they have a full ratchet and effectively get pound for pound, dollar for dollar back, their position is restored.

A weighted average ratchet may be calculated.

I won't go into the numbers here. However, to put it another way, if it's a tiny down round, the impact will be averaged out, and it'll be less of a dilution.

The investors will get fewer shares than they would if the round was large.

Now, weighted average ratchets can be narrow based (they just refer to the issued stock) or broad based (they cover also the warrants and outstanding options), which adds an extra layer of complexity to the simple situation described above.

There may be another rinky-dink in there that says they might be pay to play, which implies the investor will only profit from the anti-dilution ratchet if he or she participates to their intended level of entitlement in the round following.

There are numerous factors to consider when it comes to Antagonist dilution matches.

And, of course, this is where your attorney and solicitor will get their money.

Let's start with drag and tagging. Let's first discuss dragging.

This implies that once 50% or more of the stockholders consent to sell, the shares will sell the firm.

As a result, they can pull the remaining shareholders to the table and force them to take the same price in the same conditions, that is, the minorities don't have holdout power against the majority to prevent a sale of the firm.

And this is something BK's will want to have a finger in.

The tagalong, on the other hand, ensures that if there is a sale, I will be granted the same terms for my shares as the majority owner so that they can't sell their stocks and then leave the new control of the firm bickering and offering a less favorable deal to me.

There's one other circumstance that might be difficult, and it makes me anxious when I see it.

That is the term for SKO sale rates, which are calculated in this manner. Some shareholders might choose to sell some of their shares to a third party, but not all of them.

If the other investors have comparable sales rates, they can ask for the same terms as well.

They all get to clear something off the table at that moment. This might be a little difficult, and it could prevent liquidity events before exit.

So, from that perspective, it may be a good thing, but it is dependent on the business's arrangements and investors you have in the company.

Let's just talk about the term sheet in terms of what's legally binding and what isn't. Because at the top of the term sheet, you will undoubtedly see a clause that states "subject to contract."

However, at the bottom of it, you will find a few lines that state these sections are legally binding and pertain to confidentiality, which implies you won't tell anybody else about your involvement in negotiations.

Second, confidentiality, which means the investor has time when he's only talking to you and no one else where you can negotiate the whole investment agreement and do your research.

They'll be spending money, and they'll want to have a window of opportunity to finalize that transaction with you before competition arises.

So it will protect your privacy, and it will describe the terms of confidentiality, and you won't be able to discuss the details of the contract or even its existence.

That is something you should be aware of since confidentiality and suitability are legally enforceable.

It's now a subject of debate how long they should be allowed to enjoy exclusivity and whether or not a lengthy period is appropriate, which essentially binds you up and prevents you from accomplishing anything.

If it's too quick, they may not be able to complete the transaction. The typical duration is two to six weeks.

So that's what you don't believe is genuinely short. However, four to six weeks is typical, and you might go as long as eight weeks.

You'll also find break fees, which may include legal and other expenditures, but you should consult with your lawyer first, as these are often costly.

So this is the framework that you'll find in a term sheet. And I'm hoping that by providing you that structure, at least you have an idea of what's there and why it's there.

Of course, what you sign up for is entirely your decision and the responsibility of your legal advisors.

Chapter 52: Term Sheets: Key Concepts

I'd like to use this chapter to reemphasize certain key ideas you'll encounter in your term sheet, in order to assist them stick in your memory and help you understand them better.

The first is concerned with the valuation, and it includes everything related to the total amount of money being provided as well as the primary appraisal.

As a result, the pre money valuation serves as the basis for assessing the value of the shares and their price, which investors will pay when they make their investment.

The performance evaluation, as well as the financing amount that is provided, are part of the post-money valuation.

Look at multiples of earnings trailing revenues as a rule of thumb when adding up a company's worth. This is often known as the P/E multiple and refers to the amount of money you would pay for each dollar of profits in a stock or business.

They'll be more interested in the team's background, the size of the market and company growth prospects.

When developing a business valuation, these are the issues that will be addressed, argued, and safeguarded.

When you're dealing with a startup company that may or may not have any earnings, it's almost impossible to estimate the worth of the firm.

If you utilize a future-looking forecast, such as discounted cash flow, your calculations will be highly reliant on the assumptions you make in the future.

Forecasts for term sheets will devote a significant amount of time to the board and company management.

And one thing in particular, which can be quite complicated, is the allocation of board seats.

Having A, B, and C on your board is now considered a positive thing since they have a lot of industry knowledge and contacts as well as networks that should provide significant value.

You also want to make sure they provide actual added value to your board. However, if you end up with a board that is too big or unmanageable, it will be very difficult.

Typically, at this period of the company's history, you may need to restructure the board so that some of the original founders cede their seats and allow investors to join.

You may wind up having to accept as a founder that you may well end up losing a majority of control of the board.

That is, however, something that will be specific to your agreement and which you'll have to give careful thought.

Choose carefully who you recruit as a board member. It's not simply about the money. The contribution they can make to your company is of paramount importance.

And, of course, you want to hire the highest-quality individuals for your board.

Here are a few more pointers.

When you have an odd number of people on your board, you'll never be deadlocked and referred back to the chairman when you put something up for a vote.

Another excellent thing to have on a board is an independent director or directors, people who are not founders, but who may have a lot of industry and expertise and knowledge, who can bring a lot of value to the board while also being able to evaluate both sides of the argument when any issue is discussed, especially if it's contentious.

Liquidation preferences are concerned with how much money investors receive when something goes wrong.

And, for investors, what they're seeking to do is say, "Well, look; I'm going to make ten investments in this fund."

I'm well aware that a lot of them won't thrive, and I'm hoping for at least one or two of them to do exceptionally well.

However, for the Startups that don't do well, I'd like to try and recover as much of my original investment as feasible. The liquidation preference is there to assist you in the event of your company's bankruptcy.

They're now asking for one times liquidation preference, which is typical. So they're attempting to get a dollar for each dollar put into the fund in order to get a dollar back out of it.

That's before anybody else gets a dime out.

You can find them asking for two times liquidation preferences on occasion, which means they want to receive twice their money back for each dollar they invest.

There must be a compelling reason for you to give up your cause. Their interests might be active or inactive.

What does this signify in terms of practicality? It's fairly easy. If they don't participate, they get there and are given one-time or two-time money back, and then they do not take part in any additional distribution of what is left.

They earn their pro-rata share of the rest of the money, not just once or twice, but on a continual basis if they take part.

So, you'll want to know what the distinctions are. Essentially, one time is typical, but anything else must be examined very critically.

Now, voting rights and transfers of control may be highly contentious. And they're frequently included in the term sheet agreement as well as the classes of stock and the equity structure.

That is also reflected in the articles of association, which are frequently amended.

Typically, the founders and employees have ownership in the company's common stock. In the UK language, ordinary shares are often referred to. The preferred stock, on the other hand, might be convertible. This is a separate class of share. The investors hold it.

Those shares have diverse rights, including the right to vote and veto, which might lead to a slew of possibilities such as swamping rights, change of control, rights, dragalong whatever it is give them.

The most important point is to understand what the new class of share entails and how it compares to common stock, as well as what you're giving up.

Each stock class may have its own series; therefore, each class may be taken forward.

If you have a large investor, such as an angel or venture capitalist, he can purchase a preferred stock in the series for the next group of investors who join the firm.

Of course, the Series B will look to the previous series and try to ensure that they are protected not only against the typical, but also against the critical.

And the easiest method to do so is to avoid creating separate series in each stock class, as that will quickly get messy if you have a whole slew of various rounds.

The investor's preferred stock comes with a variety of safeguards. However, you must be aware of them since they can have a significant influence on the company's management and privileges.

Make sure you understand the distinctions between them, founder and employee vesting, which I'll continue to discuss since it's such a contentious issue. By ensuring that the entrepreneurs have to earn their stock back, investor protection is assured.

One or two items to keep in mind is that, if you have reverting rights, they signify that from the company's standpoint, if a key managerial figure is dismissed, the firm has the right to repurchase its shares at a very low price to return equity back into the business.

So, from the perspective of a manager or an entrepreneur, you need to be aware of what you're giving up here and decide with your lawyer whether you're comfortable with it.

Typically, you will receive standing standard vesting conditions. They may be the provision that you see in the terms and conditions. And if it is, you must make sure you understand what it means.

Now, in some cases, there are capitalization changes before the investment, which are not uncommon. And they may be beneficial to everyone, particularly if you have a founder who is no longer active in the company but still owns a big stake.

Bring these back in so that the workers who operate within the company can profit from them and some are merely passive, which is a huge mistake.

The original creator does not own a whole stack of value, which he has abandoned and is no longer earning.

So it's not unusual to see these equity stakes being repurchased before the investment is made, as specified in the term sheet.

These should always be factored in. It is a time-consuming procedure. It's a lengthy paper.

The aim of the term sheet is to make the investment contract easier to comprehend.

However, you must ensure that you obtain your term sheet rate because once it has been determined; it is very difficult to modify it and renegotiate the investment agreement.

Chapter 53: What Are Term Sheets Trying to Accomplish?

I'd want to explain what a term sheet is attempting to accomplish, because you need to comprehend the goals of both the investors and the company's entrepreneurs.

This will assist you in establishing the appropriate equilibrium in any talks about conditions in your term sheet.

In a term sheet, there are generally three crucial sections: concerns regarding the financing. Then there's corporate governance. Then there's what will happen if everything goes wrong.

These are the contentious issues that must be resolved and agreed when creating a term sheet and an investment.

Let's start by discussing the investor's objectives.

From the investors' standpoint, the goal is to make the most of their investment. When a firm is finally sold and they recognize their investment, they'll exit the business.

They frequently do so by converting preferred shares or, in some cases, a separate class of shares with distinct rights to the common shares.

And, to be honest with you, I'm not trying to go into too much detail. You must keep in mind that I'm attempting to provide you an overview, but technical matters differ greatly between the United Kingdom and Europe when compared to the United States.

However, the fundamentals are the same; however, the implementation is varied. So keep this in mind when looking at past experiences.

However, from an investor's standpoint, the objective is to invest and get the greatest return on his investment as possible.

The flip side is that if things don't go as planned, investors want to be able to protect their downside as much as possible and include language that would provide them with more of the downside exit than is proportional to the equity they own.

Because in those situations, it's very probable that they won't get all of their money back.

They're seeking to recoup as much of their money back as possible at the expense of the other shareholders.

They also want a voice and control, even if they have a minority position in the firm.

They do not want to be in a position where other investors may band together and attack them or dilute them, or take actions that they disagree with.

This is why they have provisions in there that allow them to veto certain corporate governance concerns.

Now, many investors want to be able to force a sale of the firm at a later date, even when they're in a minority position, simply so that you can discover an scenario where the present owners or other holders truly want to continue.

But when the office is put on the table, and the institutional investor, a series or B investor says yes, I'll take that. Thank you very much.

They want provisions in the investor agreement, as well as the term sheet, that will allow them to do so.

They're also concerned about having the company's founders and key management tightly linked to and focused on the business.

So they don't want them to start any other companies.

They want to make sure that if their shares have to reinvest, they do so in a way that is most beneficial.

It will be one of the main goals of the investors to ensure that the company's founders and key management are working hard to create money for themselves rather than getting distracted by other projects.

Let's consider the term sheet from the perspective of an entrepreneur.

What are they after?

Of course, they're seeking to raise as much money as possible without compromising the company's long-term success.

As a result, they're on the lookout for anything that would guarantee them as much money as possible, so that the share price is as high as feasible.

As a result, investors receive fewer shares and are less diluted.

They also seek to strike a balance between providing investors with the appropriate degree of protection while not sacrificing too much of the upside.

In return for joining into dilution or liquidation rights, the present investors are attempting to ensure that they receive a fair share of the profits. The current founders are attempting to ensure that they get a good chance at the upside for their risk taking as well as protecting investors on the downside by utilizing nonparticipating preferred stock, which means that investors can get their money back.

It's possible it's a one-time event. It could be two or more times, but once they've recouped their money, they don't contribute any further to the business' liquidation proceeds.

Of course, they want to retain as much power as possible. This investor is, after all, a minority stakeholder.

As a result, they will be looking to negotiate down many of these vetoes and control rates that the investors would demand.

As an entrepreneur, you should check with your lawyer or solicitor on this subject.

They will want to safeguard their own positions because if they are simply dismissed and tough leaver provisions are used against them, they will lose their equity, investment, and hard work.

It would be a complete waste of effort to put this operation together.

When term sheets are put together, entrepreneurs, founders, key managers in the firm will be looking for their own personal downside protection.

Now, of course, there are two aspects to consider.

However, the most important part of this entire negotiation is to ensure that your interests are aligned with those of the other party in order for you not to fight against one another because they have different incentive to get a unique outcome.

So you're really trying to tie the founding team and key management together, so that they can align themselves with choices and be found to share in order to have an upside from these warrants or options, which will motivate them to keep working hard on the company.

The vetoes and tagalong attempts are there to ensure that no one may force the sale of the firm until adequate value is created, which will allow everyone a fair profit.

So, if you have one dissident stockholder and it might be a financial investor with a separate objective, he might have an agenda. For the same reason, you genuinely want to attempt and establish these checks and balances so that they can't harm you in any way.

Now, the vesting schedule is intended to link the company, its executives and managers, as well as other stakeholders, in order to ensure their loyalty.

That's probably not in the interests of shareholders if they've acquired all their shares and can walk away with them or if they suddenly decide to try to sell the firm early.

So, again, there's more to some of these procedures than simply appearing to penalize one participant over the other.

The whole goal of the intellectual property assignments is to ensure that the company's intellectual property does not fall into the hands of its founders, thus allowing them to devote their efforts to the firm.

They're not concentrated on pursuing their own personal agenda. And, once again, this is critical in terms of achieving alignment right now.

Don't forget to add the end date. It's a negotiation if you reach a point in your business when you're running out of cash and only have one investor at the table, giving him an advantage in the negotiation.

As an entrepreneur, as a founder, as a management portion of the management team, you should be in a position where you have many term sheets on the table and can select among them. The power, balance of power in the negotiation will be on your side of the table if you can put yourself in a spot where you have several term papers to fallback.

However, at the end of the day, my recommendation is not to be too greedy and to look for an agreement that everyone is satisfied with.

If you go into an agreement with the assumption that if you do this, I'm going to get a benefit and I'm not going to have anything at all in return, then you're definitely going to have a bad relationship.

So those are the things I'd want you to consider, because if you know what she's attempting to accomplish, it will be easier for you to have an unbiased perspective with regards to the negotiation nitty gritty.

Section 9 | LOI in Mergers and Acquisitions

Chapter 54: LOIs and MOUs Introduction

I'd like to walk you through this area on Letters of Intent, LOI's, and memorandum of understanding.

The most essential feature about these papers is that there isn't a single correct solution.

There is no such thing as a one-size-fits-all document that can simply be pulled off the shelf and claimed to be what we require. Every deal situation has its own architecture, requirements, and negotiation hotspots.

You must also comprehend that you will not receive a one-size-fits-all solution for how to create one of these items.

So. Now, having made that point, I don't want you to believe that because you've gone through this, you can write an LOI or an MOU. You may have a decent idea of what goes in them, but you will not have the legal knowledge or information to produce a good legal document.

This book and material is not intended to turn you into a lawyer. It's designed to provide you with an insight into the subject as well as information for research purposes only.

Leave everything else to your attorney or lawyer, who should write and draw up the documents.

The point, though, is that I want you to understand what goes into the paper regardless.

What should go into an LOI, and what you may not need to include in a different way if you have a firm grasp on the many alternatives available to you and say that yes, we require this, this is something we need. We don't require anything else. Nothing more is required.

Not only that, but you should also leave with a clear understanding of why that particular passage is there.

What is the aim of that sentence and paragraph? It's also critical to keep in mind that M&A practices in the United States and the United Kingdom are very different.

And I'll provide you a few more examples between the United Kingdom and the United States later on.

You'll notice how the letter's styles are extremely varied, but you'll also observe that it makes use of distinct language. However, many points are surprisingly similar.

Of course, law varies from jurisdiction to jurisdiction. Because of these variances, the application of the US law and, more particularly, state legislation in the United States varies.

The legal systems of the United Kingdom and Europe are vastly different. As a result, you could have a restriction in one jurisdiction that is acceptable but illegal in another state.

To summarize, you must be aware of the legislation.

Now, I'm going to do my best to describe the stuff. I'll show you some examples.

I'll provide you with some checklists and my thorough notes, including any relevant case studies.

Hopefully, this will provide you a deeper understanding of what goes into a letter of intent and why it is important.

That concludes the stage setting, if you choose.

I'd want you to grasp the background and goal of this section.

With that knowledge, hopefully you'll be able to get a lot out of this material about letters of intent and memorandums.

Chapter 55: MOUs and LOIs in Mergers and Acquisitions

A letter of intent, LOI or Memorandum of Understanding is a legal document that outlines the terms and conditions of a potential business deal. These phrases are interchangeable: MOU, LOI, and MOU.

This letter allows both parties to express their commitment to making a deal and desire for more talks.

The LOI is a document that outlines the key terms of the proposed agreement to ensure there is genuine agreement on critical issues.

This is the fundamental and most important component of a transaction, upon which all other elements are built. This is when relationships of trust are established that lead to profitable transactions.

An LOI can be broken down into two categories: a long form and a short form.

A short negotiating letter should be used to cover the basic points of the transaction, which gives negotiations momentum and direction.

This list includes the following headings: an introduction, a transaction overview and structure, and an example timetable.

Contractual non-disclosures and the need for confidentiality are among the prerequisites for a successful due diligence effort. These are among the core parameters of an LOI.

The MOU serves as the foundation for writing the sale and purchase agreement, and it can also be used to write a development agreement.

It's also important to remember that there were four components to any trade, including operational staff, finances, and law. The LOI is used to define the criteria for all of these elements in the deal under debate.

Chapter 56: LOI's Binding or Non-Binding?

Is it a legally enforceable contract, or is it simply a non-binding agreement?

Offers are available on a subject-to-contract and due diligence basis. The LOI can be either binding or non-binding, and if it's non-binding, the term "non-binding," "subject to contract and due diligence," or some other similar phrase must be used so that the reader understands that the offer is binding.

In most LOI s, there are only a few binding obligations, with two significant exceptions.

Both parties must keep confidential the fact that discussions are underway and a deal is being discussed, and confidentiality agreements should be established before disclosing substantial amounts of sensitive data early in the transaction.

Exclusive, or no shop agreement is another term for exclusivity.

When the seller says that she or he will not talk with another party or utilize the talks as a bargaining tool to get a better deal from someone else,

If you're a private owner, add that the seller must continue to run the firm in the usual course of business.

It's a good idea to include a statement to the effect that the binding provisions are the entire agreement between the parties, superseding or including previous oral or written agreements, and that no modifications may be made without both parties' signatures.

Chapter 57: The Benefits and Drawbacks of LOIs

I'd like to go over the advantages and drawbacks, as well as the benefits and disadvantages of LOI's, right now.

The LOI specifies the boundaries for future bargaining. It also forms the basis for drafting and negotiating a final agreement.

Unless I'm able to save money while also being able to use it as a bargaining chip by either side.

It can be used to back up an application for funding from a third party, such as a bank, with adequate disclosure to the seller.

It has the potential to build trust between the parties.

It may act as a starting point for the buyer's due diligence, which usually entails fees.

It may also be used to seal off a section of the basement as an exclusive realm. The most important benefit for a buyer is that they can gain this exclusivity and have a reasonable confidence that a transaction will succeed on fair terms before investing further time and money, particularly in due diligence, according to some experts.

For the seller, exclusivity is a disadvantage since it creates uncertainty about the terms of a potential deal. However, they also benefit from increased clarity on those terms.

A buyer can also receive a written quote, making it more difficult for them to change their minds afterward.

The cash-out provision also puts pressure on the buyer, who must complete the transaction subject to due diligence and contract drafting before the expiration of the exclusivity period.

The disadvantages of LOI's. They might become a time sink.

They may also result in notification requirements for customers, creditors, suppliers, government agencies, and others.

Even if the goal is to be non-binding, they may become binding.

Finally, be precise about why you're doing an LOI when you do one. It's usually better not to conduct an LOI if there isn't a need for it.

Chapter 58: The Key Components of LOIs Part 1

The following are the major components of LOI's first part:

In no event should the data presented in this book be considered legal counsel and it should only be utilized in conjunction with the help of a competent corporate tax lawyer or solicitor.

Parties to the transaction. These aspects of the letter describe how two business sides of a transaction are buying one another and on what terms, including the structure, purpose, and scale of the deal.

It's critical to clarify the names of the corporate entities involved in the transaction, as well as any listing company numbers or places of incorporation in case there is a future dispute.

It's critical that you get these specifics correct.

The contract is then summarized in a few sentences.

This part of the contract details the purchase cost and terms, including the total purchase price and the currency.

The terms of the payment may include a down payment, promissory notes, interest rate default circumstances, and so on. Performance payments can be earned out as well as royalty fees, purchase price adjustments, assumptions and adjustment events, and liabilities to be assumed.

It will also indicate the allocation of the purchase price, depending on your agreement.

If due diligence reveals that the initial valuation based on the company's financial records was incorrect, it may be appropriate to add a revised basis for calculating the company's value.

If the buyer accepts your price, then you'll have a chance to renegotiate it.

Forecast EBITDA, any ad banks to EBITDA for one-offs or vendor drawings, due diligence, and supporting the achievement of the company's forecasts are all potential key assumptions underlying a valuation.

The statement that the firm has adequate net assets at completion to support its regular working capital and operational needs, as well as no significant contracts or other such arrangements ending or changing badly as a consequence of the acquisition.

The LOI should spell out the buyer's plans to keep the selling company's management and employees on their current employment contracts.

The event of senior or specialist people leaving a company without being required to continue working there. This should be explicitly stated.

It is critical to disclose that a manager may depart the firm on a sale. To prevent any future employment termination disputes, this issue must be handled correctly.

What are the future responsibilities of the management team? The buyer will, for the most part, wish to secure the services and loyalty of senior staff in a letter of intent.

The first step to doing this is to make a clear statement of their future roles in the preceding paragraph.

Chapter 59: The Key Components of LOIs - Part 2

The next sets of key components of LOIs are discussed in this part.

The purchase agreement is the next thing to glance at. The alleyway may describe the company's primary goals in the sale and purchase agreement, as well as any restrictions or limitations on its rights, assets, or liabilities.

It should be made clear in the letter that the offer is subject to a definitive sale and purchase agreement's signing.

It's also possible that the parties involved in a deal may be able to renegotiate it at some point. In cases like these, it might be good for the buyer to make sure they have enough money set aside and where they're getting it from.

The paperwork should also make it clear that the agreement is dependent on warranties and indemnities from relevant parties, which may become unavailable.

Due diligence review. The manner in which the scope of the due diligence review is defined may be broad or detailed, such as some of the following cases.

This may include an examination of year-to-date results, a current run rate for the company, projected outcomes for the current full year sales analysis and profitability by customer analysis of the existing pipeline assessment of key assumptions for the next financial year.

Forecasts predicted the market's growth and a firm's position in the market, as well as expansion potential into new product areas and international markets.

Investigate current customer relationships and talks with important client contacts. There may also be provisions for particular commercial, legal, and environmental investigation.

A timetable should be included in the closing. A timetable might be prepared to detail the main activities to be completed between the signing of the LOI and the completion of the transaction.

This clause may be referred back to if the buyer's demands for documentation, information, or personnel are not met by the seller.

The schedule might look something like this, with a two-week period for preliminary research followed by an eight-week period of exclusivity, including the formal due diligence time.

This will also include the drafting of legal paperwork, including a sale and purchase agreement.

You may go on to note that the timetable's accomplishment might be contingent on timely information receipt, and you may want to append a timetable with the main deliverables and milestones, as well as a target completion date, to the paper.

Let's look at four of the most important terms in this potentially non-binding letter, starting with exclusivity.

The buyer will request that the seller grant them exclusivity in order to deter them from discussing a deal with anybody else.

It will have an end date on it and is generally between six and eight weeks in duration, however longer timeframes may be agreed depending on the seller's interests.

Confidentiality must be maintained. Both parties agree to keep information about the agreement to themselves and only a few persons within the two enterprises, but their respective professional advisers.

In a deal between two private companies, this is especially crucial. This clause prohibits public disclosure of the negotiations and agreement parties outside either company's consumers or lenders, for example, from being informed of the discussions.

If LOI is binding, you may want to add a paragraph that explains the terms and situations under which the contract can be terminated in the event of a termination event; there may be a clause for a breakup if you include such information.

However, this may not be the only option in the case of a seller's breach.

It's common for each side to pay their own costs and expenses in a deal like this.

A termination fee is any charge made by a seller to a buyer in order to end the transaction. A break-up fee is one of these fees. If the deal does not close as expected due to certain factors, such as failure of consideration or nonpayment, the parties may agree that the seller will pay the buyer a breakup fee.

This is to ensure that the seller remains committed throughout the bargaining, and the buyer is attempting to avoid having to pay large deal fees that are not linked to the transaction's completion.

The entire clause will be binding, even if certain provisions are non-binding in a non-binding LOI. As we've seen, even though some clauses are non-binding in a non-binding LOI, there will still be other clauses that are binding.

There should be no purpose of establishing legal relations. This is a belt and braces clause meant to underscore the non-binding nature of the correspondence.

With the aforementioned exceptions, the following words may take on one of the following meanings:

This letter is simply meant to serve as a pre-contractual agreement, and it will not and may not be used as the basis for any legal relationship between the parties who do not wish to establish one.

As I previously stated, a designation of negotiators is necessary. This can describe the principles, the participants in the talks as well as their contact information.

The objective is to provide all information about the talks to those people covered in the text.

If any individuals are replaced, a replacement will be made. The method to accomplish this is usually specified in writing.

Applicable law: This clause will state that the offer is non-binding and interpreted in accordance with, say, English or wherever the transaction is taking place, specifies the jurisdiction and venue for any future disputes related to the LOI.

And now we get to the end of an LOI, where I'll explain why in an M&A situation and hope that this explanation and clause-by-clause walkthrough will be useful to you as you study the constituent parts, or components, of an LOI.

Chapter 60: A Sample of a UK Style LOI

I'd now like to provide you with an illustration of a U.K. style letter of intent.

The significance of this letter is that it is not meant to be a comprehensive document.

There is no definitive answer. This is a case study for me, and it's only illustrative.

That's a template from one of my library's books, and it's probably one of the greatest ones I've ever seen. I'm hoping you'll find the information useful, but I don't want to offer you some of my precedents because they are one-time deals and pertain to real transactions.

Second, because there are so many different variations and some clauses contradict one another, the whole situation becomes very perplexing.

So, therefore, if you've got a contract with a straight down payment, you can't have provisions for both in the same document.

This is a template that is meant to be used as a basis for further development. And hopefully, by looking at it, you'll get an idea of the type of letter and the subject matter.

So we'll take a look at that. I've included a PDF of this letter with this chapter as a service to you.

So here we are. You may see the letter set out, which is designed to look like a letter from the United States.

Take a somewhat different approach. Please note the warning, which is crucial. This is for educational and instructive purposes only.

You start off with an introduction, which informs the reader that the terms' heads are not intended to be legally enforceable.

How much money is spent on the rehab? How much would you have to spend?

The consequences of this are explained, as well.

Other important phrases: These are transaction-specific terms, as well as due diligence and additional permissions.

The deal will incorporate an exchange of cash. The acquiring company might also need to secure shareholder approval for the transaction. There may be regulatory, takeover code, or monopoly concerns that must be addressed in the transaction and that form conditions precedent.

Exclusivity.

We've discussed a lot of confidentiality. We've mentioned some expenses, as well as any paperwork that must be reviewed.

We're looking at the first draft of the sale and purchase agreement in this instance.

It's all about the details in this scenario, including the purchase of assets or an asset purchase agreement, timetable, legal matters, and third-party rights.

So you'll understand that it's structured in an organized way. It's simple to go back to numbered paragraphs and headings.

And, as I mentioned earlier, it's largely the same material.

What I would suggest you do is sit down with your lawyer and make a list of things to cover first.

What do we need to include?

Chapter 61: An Sample of a US-Style LOI

Now, I'd like to discuss with you an example of a typical U.S.-style letter of intent.

The first thing I'd like you to notice in a US style letter is that it has a distinct style, which is quite unusual.

There's a short introductory rubric, and then it's a straightforward list of items.

It's a lot more practical, and it's much more legally written.

That's excellent because it means you'll be much more certain and that working with your lawyer is a must. The point is that it's a template. It's an example. It's not supposed to be a one-size-fits-all document in any case.

It's only intended to provide you an idea of how these papers might appear and what to anticipate.

Let's go over it and examine a typical document structure now.

It starts with a set of introductory rubrics that explain what's going on. Then it goes into a very detailed description of what's going on, from start to finish.

So we begin by discussing the transaction structure, stock exchange ratio, consideration, and rights of board representation. It's also made very clear that it's a shared concern with the fact that it's called a "shared consideration." The target firm's employee stock options are treated in this case, which is crucial.

Other concerns, such as confidentiality and binding representations and warranties, are all equally essential.

We'll go down to page three in the closing conditions.

Prior to the close of a merger or acquisition, there are provisions that must be satisfied. These are conditions precedent that include voting agreement and proxy termination costs, as well as timing and diligence expenses.

There's a section on the board of directors and business strategy, which I'm sure you're all very familiar with, but there are still a few that are coming in for the first time and are most likely seeing them for the first time.

There is a lot to cover when it comes to shareholder voting and proxy.

However, I emphasize once again that each case is unique and must be evaluated individually.

You'll need to go over your lists of points you want to communicate with your lawyer, meet with some knowledgeable people who have written similar documents, and construct the document.

Hopefully, you're beginning to develop a decent sense for how these papers are constructed.

But I emphasize once again that the most important thing is that you know what you need in your document and why you want it there.

Chapter 62: Summary and Additional Resources

I'd like to bring this section of LOIs and MOUs to a close, so let's take a look at everything we've discussed.

As well as some additional resources, I'd like to draw your attention to a few more.

The significant objective of this section on letters of intent, a memorandum of understanding, is for you to know what a letter of intent entails.

You can also discuss terms with them, and they'll explain to you what goes in and why it's there.

The goal isn't to enable you to produce your own letter, but rather to give you the knowledge so that you may collaborate with your legal consultant in order to develop the letter and document you require for your transaction.

We've looked at the reasons why LOIs are significant, as well as how they work.

We discussed the pros and cons of being binding or non-binding, and they may be either. Even in non-binding writings, there are binding clauses and we've seen how they function.

I've outlined the benefits and drawbacks of an LOI so you can determine whether or not one is really required.

Then I've gone through the main parts of letters of intent in some detail. That is complemented with two distinct chapters.

I'm going to walk you through everything step by step and give you some resources so that you can fully comprehend what's going on.

Then we've looked at a UK example letter and a US example letter, both of which should help you understand how the words in those letters are defined.

Before I depart, I'd like to leave you with a checklist of questions that you may use to visit your attorneys or solicitors and determine whether they are required. And I'll also share with you some of my in-depth notes so that you may go over them later.

Hopefully, you'll find those useful as reference materials. That concludes our overview of letters of intent and use memorandum of understanding. I hope you now have a better grasp on what these are, why you need them, and why particular clauses are included in them that they do.

Section 10: The Due Diligence Procedure

Chapter 63: Due Diligence: What is It and Why Is it Important?

Due diligence is a term that's frequently used but rarely understood. It's a phrase that implies care and attention, but it doesn't tell us what exactly due diligence means or why it's so important.

As a buyer, it is your duty to thoroughly inspect what you're buying throughout the process. The seller will be there for you, and it is reasonable to expect.

Don't take his word for it; be cautious, especially since he or she appears to be well-informed on the subject. But don't assume he's telling you the truth, not hiding anything significant, and providing you with all you need for your detailed study, including answering any queries that may emerge from your investigation.

It might take anything from six to 12 weeks for thorough due diligence, and it's frequently a lot more time-consuming for Public firms.

What are the benefits of conducting thorough research?

Due diligence is the process of obtaining information about a company and its assets so that the buyer may fully understand what he/she is purchasing. The buyer must learn as much as possible in the restricted time available to identify any unknown risks, as well as to verify what he has been told about the firm.

The vendor will have a greater level of understanding about the strengths and limitations of their product or service.

The closing statement will also contain the documents and evidence needed to establish the representations and warranties in the sale and purchase agreement.

What information do they want?

All things considered, the buyer's advisers are responsible for providing all of the information requested by the seller. In most cases, this includes a request for a copy of most if not all of the company's documentation, including its memorandum and articles of association, recent audited financial statements and current business plans and forecasts, as well as tax returns and information

The client's complete business records, including employment contracts, personnel files, information on employee benefits and pension plans, material sales agreements, supplier contracts and distribution agreements, licensing arrangements, intellectual property issues and all real estate agreements and deeds.

A financial audit typically includes the following questions: What is the firm's income statement? How did you generate it? What were your expenses in coming up with this figure? Who are your largest customers and investors? If a company has no major suppliers or distribution channels that aren't known to the public, a list of supplementary inquiries will be added.

There is no such thing as a typical document since each company is distinct, and the initial questions should be tailored to the specific needs of each deal scenario, with real estate companies being far more varied than software firms. Due diligence by advisers looking at environmental concerns, customers, and suppliers may well be necessary in addition to accountants and attorneys.

The market and technology will provide you with lists of information requirements.

This chapter provides an explanatory brief of the complete due diligence checklist, which is only intended to assist you understand what needs to be done and why.

As part of this chapter, you'll find an outline of the accounting scope of work as a downloadable PDF.

Chapter 64: Use Virtual Data Rooms to Your Advantage

In the 1980s, a data room was a physical location. It was commonly located at the business's lawyers' office, though it might also be found at the company itself.

Running the program in a secure area was also not an option, as there were many files to compile and transport to the room, only for them to be physically turned up at the other end.

Whether you're visiting a new city or country, retaining track of your personal documents is essential. It's not unusual to discover hidden skeletons while rummaging through paperwork looking for a fresh start.

Virtual data rooms, which are now the standard, allow data to be gathered much quicker and shared securely on a global basis with minimal disruption for both parties.

They're also beneficial to privacy since they prevent the target firm's employees from being disrupted out of their routines for weeks on end, leading to rumors and anxiety among them.

If you're creating a process, make sure your firm starts building the virtual data room as soon as possible so that it doesn't get in the way of the process.

If you can just give certain information, the less sensitive stuff before the LOI is signed to allow your counterparty to make some progress on due diligence before this historic event, you may be able to negotiate better terms or remove conditions from the LOI.

The buyer will find it a lot easier to manage and absorb information if it is provided in accordance with their standard procedure. Early on, consider whose due diligence list you should use: the buyer will have an easier time managing and absorbing information if it is delivered in line with their usual practice.

The seller may have already prepared their information in accordance with their advisors' standards and be hesitant to reorder it all for one counterparty.

Private businesses have different standards than public firms, but there's one more stage to the procedure.

There are a number of additional disclosures that public companies must make, which are then available for review by the general public, but private firms are not subjected to these disclosure rules, therefore the list is likely to be much longer.

Chapter 65: People Management - Processes

A buy team should spend at least a day going over all the deal points with the whole team before signing an LOI.

Your goal should be to establish levels of materiality and identify the key issues that prevent you from closing the deal.

What approach are you planning on taking?

Do you intend to push aggressively or take a more cautious approach?

As the other side provides critical confidential information and you don't want to give up your concessions too soon, your negotiating position may shift.

It's critical to keep the list of deal issues as brief as feasible if required, but if you don't have one, make a longer list of B points that you want confirmed in due diligence.

Don't forget that many of the most contentious issues concern crucial posts and what will happen to high-level workers after the acquisition is completed, get these things resolved as soon as possible.

This will not, of course, address the problems of personality. When Strong astute executives try to impose their viewpoint on a transaction in order to fulfill their own interests rather than contribute to the entire deal, this won't help.

It's usually better to sort out the people issues before you spend a lot of money on due diligence, only to discover that they're unsolvable.

Chapter 66: Key Takeaways from Our Process of Doing Deep Due Diligence

Now I'd like to go through the key takeaways from this portion of the due diligence process.

Discovery and verification are the heart of due diligence; it's about unearthing skeletons in the closet, ensuring that you've been told the truth by your competition.

It's not enough to believe them. You must actually go and verify that everything they've said is correct.

To accomplish so, you must first get them to provide the supporting evidence to back up what they have told you.

It is a very detailed time-Consuming, expensive but critical process.

Caveat emptor, which means Buyer beware in Latin, the seller is ecstatic as long as they sell and sign a purchase agreement, because the risk is all on your side and you must ensure that you understand the company you're buying as well as the person selling it, which necessitates that you truly comprehend all of the risks involved with the deal.

It's important to remember that the data discovered via due diligence is used in the negotiation of a sale and purchase agreement, so you can fine-tune the conditions if required.

Because you can utilize the information you provided, you may renegotiate critical elements of the agreement. It was incorrect.

Let's examine it again, go back to it and look at it once more. And in the worst-case scenario, if something truly terrible happens, walk away and cut your losses.

It's better to walk away before you make a bad agreement than it is to go down the road of disaster.

Remember, it's all about information. You can't be too thorough.

You must accumulate a large number of lists that concentrate on various aspects of the business, such as sales and marketing.

So you must cover all of the legal documents and financial information, as well as anything else about the company's operations that involves consumers, suppliers, or dealers.

Now, I've given you some templates to get you started, but they simply take you so far.

There is no such thing as an ideal template since every transaction is extremely distinctive.

Make sure you turn to your advisors, get the information or the starting points from their template, and utilize their experience to help you ensure that you submit the greatest high-quality information requests possible.

It's all about controlling the process, so make sure you get organized and prepared for your negotiation strategy as well as your negotiation strategy meeting. This is critical. Also, remember that management issues may be the most contentious. So don't overlook them or put them off until later.

Finally, be aware of powerful personalities with their own personal agendas who are normally concerned with position, money, perks, choices, and make sure you have a handle on them so they don't distort the bargaining process and their interests don't make life more difficult for everyone else.

So those are the major points in this section on due diligence. I hope it's given you a lot of food for thought.

Chapter 67: Virtual Data Room - Activity

For task two, I want you to ensure that you're on top of the virtual data room problem and that the virtual data room is fully ready before beginning the whole due diligence procedure.

Now, let's be realistic. This should have been nearly completed before you signed the LOI.

If you're on the selling side, you've already spent a lot of time building your data room. Even if you haven't yet uploaded it to a virtual data room, you should already have it.

If you haven't, you are lagging behind the curve. And this will be a major concern in the next stage. You must address it immediately.

So as the buyer, you must ensure that the seller and their advisors have loaded all of the data and that all of the advisors, whether you're buying or selling, have had their say on what information should be gathered and compiled in digital form.

Don't worry if you haven't yet uploaded it; the actual process is simple. Make sure all of your data is ready, and that it's securely stored on one of your servers so that you may upload it.

This activity, this virtual data, is on the verge of closing the transaction. It's critical that you're informed on this.

Make sure any side you're on that the virtual data room is operational so you can really dive in.

So that's the second step in this campaign. It's ensuring that the virtual data room is completely and comprehensively prepared so that buyers and their advisors may inspect it when they come in.

Section 11 | What is Negotiation and How Does It Work?

Chapter 68: What is Negotiation?

In this chapter, I'd like to ask a simple question: what is a negotiation?

It's rather simple: two or more parties, both of which have something the other wants.

Now, in order to have that trade, both parties must consent. And negotiation is all about the back and forth negotiating.

Now, the process of negotiation may be classified into three easy phases.

The first of these is planning.

So, before you begin negotiating, do your homework.

Second, there's the whole business negotiation process.

Finally, there's the closing of the negotiation to ensure that you get the outcome you desire.

It's also critical to double-check that your counterpart has done so as well.

Simply said, that's all there is to it. That explains everything there is to know about negotiations from a bird's eye view. I'm looking forward to seeing you again in the following chapter.

Chapter 69: Negotiation Fundamentals

In this chapter, I'd like to delve deeper into some of the fundamental principles of negotiation. Let's look at how we define success since it's crucial.

In a good negotiation, you'll either reach a win-win situation or fail to finalize the agreement and end up with a lose-lose scenario.

But, you should not aim to come out on top in a win-lose situation, because if the other party walks away from the table with their objectives unfulfilled, you'll either have to accept that this agreement falls apart or suffer through a miserable relationship.

To achieve a win-win solution, you must be well prepared.

Let's take a look at some of the essential negotiation abilities you'll need.

To begin with, it's critical to make a list of goals.

These are the goals you want to achieve during the negotiation.

However, you must also have an open mind and be prepared to consider options as the negotiation progresses.

Ideas and suggestions from the other side may surface, which you haven't considered, and you must be receptive to considering how they might assist you in achieving your goals.

Prepare to be interactive; a good negotiation is one in which both sides provide each other with enough information to make an informed decision.

It's hard to have a rapport and relationship with the other side if you just sit there stone-faced.

Make sure you're focusing on your goals' items with crystal clarity. Understand what you truly care about and are willing to give up in order to get it, as well as what you're not prepared to concede.

The first stage in negotiating is to be optimistic and focus on the benefits you receive in a situation, whether it's a counterproposal from the other side or part of your own negotiation strategy in order to achieve your goals.

When you start focusing on losing things and taking a negative attitude toward negotiation, it's already the first step toward failure.

It's critical to understand the other party's requirements if you can figure out what matters most to them, and if you're oblivious to their priorities, you'll assist them in achieving their goals and get there yourself.

What's more, you can't tell whether you're creating something that will be critical to you or unimportant to them.

So, in order to properly execute your campaign, you must first understand the other side's needs and demands.

You must be willing to compromise, but you can do so in accordance with your own goals, and getting an agreement in a negotiation isn't all about standing your ground before agreeing to it.

There must be a two-way mechanism. If you know where you're heading, you can create your approach and how you'll get there.

You may actually figure out how you'll get to where you want to go.

If you're inexperienced in negotiations, consider employing agents, but if you do so, be certain to clearly define their role and ensure they understand your goals and requirements fully.

Chapter 70: Value Exchange Principle

In this chapter, I'll go through some of the most essential principles of value exchange.

To do this, I'd like to look at the major phases of a negotiation, which are preparation, proposal, debate, bargaining, and finally conclusion. The work you do before you begin a discussion with the other side is called preparation.

The first part of that discussion is usually a agenda that has been effectively proposed by both sides.

So you know how near or far apart you are after establishing the openings on both sides.

This necessitates a discussion about the relative positions, advantages and objectives.

That, of course, is a negotiating process at the end of which you hope to reach an agreement that will result in a successful transaction. There are certain fundamental elements to consider as part of this bargaining procedure.

Now, we've already discussed Win-win, but I'd want to emphasize it once again.

The goal of this negotiation is to get both of you to achieve your goals.

However, you should be aware that when dealing with someone else, there may be cultural differences, which means they may interpret what you say and do in a different way than you intended.

This is especially important when you're negotiating on a cross-border exchange.

You must also be aware of the distinctions that culture may make in each continent, as well as the cultural differences between America and Europe.

Don't assume I'm negotiating with an American and that we'll be able to communicate, since I'm British. We may or may not have a similar cultural attitude.

When you enter into the Middle East or Asia, these differences become even more obvious in negotiations.

It's critical that you remain flexible in order to adhere to these principles of exchange.

So if new facts come up, you must be prepared to modify your thinking and stance.

A balance of power exists in every negotiation. Now, the objective of this exercise is not to completely dominate the other side; rather, if you lose control of the negotiation, you may find yourself being forced to give up points that you don't want to.

So, remember this at all times. This has an impact on the way you communicate, act, and react to the other side in a negotiation.

Don't be hasty when engaging in negotiations with someone. Don't make any decisions quickly.

It's frequently more beneficial to hear the other side's entire argument on issues they want rather than conceding things point by point, since you must figure out what's important to them in the round and then what you're willing to give up in order for them to achieve their goals.

Now, understand that as a negotiator or salesperson it's necessary to know how to give concessions in order to win concessions. So don't jump into things and don't be lured into making compromises by point-for-point here the complete position of the other side before you make any concessions or responses, and finally make sure you've established clear priorities.

Chapter 71: Negotiation Objectives

In this chapter, I'd like to zoom in on your objectives and specifically how you rank them.

First and foremost, let's consider how you go about defining your goals, first of all think carefully about what you want to achieve in the negotiation.

Now, bear in mind that you may have more than one aim. If that's the case, then you should make a list of everything.

Everything that comes to mind that may be a detailed point you wish to get out of the goals and out of the negotiations.

So you make a list of all these goals, then try to rank them in terms of importance.

Understand the difference between wants and needs. Things that you want are nice to have items, but things that you need are positions that are key to your negotiating position and must be maintained.

That's why it's essential to grasp and distinguish between a customer's wants and needs.

Then, finally, consider what the opposing side's wants, needs, priorities, and objectives will be in the negotiation as you're going through it.

To assist you determine or discover what you believe is vital to them,

Now, keep an open mind on this because you may discover that you misjudged those priorities once you begin conversing with them.

However, it is critical to do this exercise as part of your preparation for the negotiation.

Let's take a closer look at how you can categorize your priorities.

To begin, you must consider this in a three-step process: first, what is the ideal, utopian end result of a negotiation from your viewpoint?

So, if you can get everything you desire, obtain all you wish for, and have all you require, what will the conclusion be?

The second step back from this is that you'll have to make concessions in some areas. What's a reasonable standpoint?

You'll be able to stay focused on your priorities and objectives as you focus down on what you're prepared to give up or in one particular sequence.

Finally, you must be explicit about your baseline position.

What is the furthest point from which you are unwilling to retreat? And if you don't have this boundary in mind before going into a deal, you're likely to be pressured into accepting terms that are below your baseline, things that are absolutely crucial to you.

So you must establish a baseline position, which is a walk away posture.

If you can't do this, you should stop negotiations immediately.

Now, to balance that out, you should keep in mind that in negotiation, being realistic is crucial. You're essentially attempting to force them to accept something less than what they were planning on offering under the guise of being reasonable.

So you must have this realism in your approach.

Second, it's critical to consider carefully before taking a stance in the negotiation that this position is not a total no-no for the other side, because doing so will set you on track to an unsuccessful bargain.

That's all there is to it for this chapter, and I hope you enjoy the next one.

Section 12: Processes for Negotiation and Transaction Management

Chapter 72: Negotiation Theory

The principle behind negotiation theory, according to which a rational argument can be set out to overcome an emotion-driven mindset, is that every arrangement may be negotiated between reasonable human beings.

The system is made up of four essential components.

One separates the fundamental urges of a person from the problem in order to focus on the other side's interests rather than his or her own.

To come to a conclusion, individuals should work together to investigate win-win alternatives and establish agreed standards for evaluating these options.

The assumption was that both sides were acting rationally and attempting to improve their negotiation outcomes.

It was, therefore, only natural that a settlement might be found in the middle ground through negotiation, with the parties' bargaining skills determining who emerges as the winner.

This concept was eventually based on a logical approach, resulting in the acronym BTA.

This is your walkaway point, and every side should be aware of it before we begin.

If you recognize this, you can utilize it to help you dominate the debates.

ZOPA: The area of potential agreement, which considers a more optimistic perspective and looks for areas of potential agreement between the parties to be successful, you must be aware of your negotiating counterpart's interests and goals.

If you can frame your proposals to satisfy his more essential wants in the negotiation while minimizing the concessions on your major issues, a mutual settlement may be reached.

Negotiating style.

Essentially, there are two types of obliques: hard and soft. Obliques that are hard focus more on getting the job done; they are strong negotiators who take an adversarial approach. Softening is more accommodating and compromising in focus, as opposed to taking a confrontational attitude.

When hard negotiators encounter soft negotiators, the outcome is that hard negotiators win but at the expense of long-term damage to their relationship with the other side.

In these circumstances, the conciliatory negotiators reach a settlement, yet they leave with the feeling that they have lost the discussion.

Chapter 73: Negotiation Preparation

Negotiation preparation.

Soldiers in the military frequently used the six P's as a personality test: Preparedness, Planning, Presence, Performance, Professionalism, and Personal integrity.

This is also true in M&A negotiations. Carry out a SWAT strengths, weaknesses, opportunities and threats analysis on both sides before beginning the negotiation process.

Examine the target firm's assets and liabilities, as well as any potential market risks. Make a thorough valuation of the company.

Whether you're buying or selling use ideas to support your evaluation, and then establish a clear picture of the company's value drivers and fixed values.

Decide your start bid and walk away price from the beginning. Only make adjustments if you are given significant new information or there is a significant change in some aspect of the company.

There are five primary tactics that you may employ to combat this. One of the most effective is to counter by establishing your own price level, which makes it more likely that they will accept a lower offer than if you had just offered them one and left it up to them whether or not to take it. This also helps prevent your tactic from being distorted.

Is it more likely that the buyers and sellers will fulfill their obligations under the contract? Do you think there's a good chance that the buyer and seller will keep their promises?

Is the buyer prepared to pay a high price for the property? How badly does he or she want it? Does he or she need to buy it as quickly as possible?

Understanding the forces that drive your target's need will help you figure out where you can apply pressure to help the transaction reach its intended conclusion.

Finally, get to know your adversary. Knowledge of their approach and tactics will help you prepare defenses against their anticipated attacks on you.

This is how you would go about studying your opponent in a game of chess. If you can contact people who have interacted with and against your counterparty in the past to learn what you can, though you must do so without breaking confidentiality or giving the game away.

Chapter 74: Management of Transaction Processes

In each transaction negotiation, there are challenging topics to be discussed and debated in advance. Combine the two sides' key alpha and beta concerns with a quick analysis of the situation for a more thorough picture.

Consider the view you have on the position, as well as any compromises or range of choices you may be prepared to table at a later time.

Create a list of these for all the concerns that are critical to you and have your team go through them.

In this example, both sides make concessions to maintain a process of reciprocity. In return for some concession on the other side, work to achieve a procedure of collaboration, negotiation, and compromise is met with some sort of give from the opposing side.

In some areas, establishing this may be difficult, as I've discovered when conducting cross-border transactions.

This must be established early on in the procedure, and it's important to argue for this as part of the process.

It follows that if a settlement is reached and agreed to, neither side should seek further concessions.

It can help to create momentum to the deal if you can establish this give-and-take approach.

Do not negotiate one issue at a time before you have a complete picture of the other side's viewpoint, then get them to make their case in full and go back and deal with matters after having an accurate knowledge of the counterparty standpoint.

You can't tell which side is more significant or unimportant in the dispute.

Take care with the timetable. There should be a deadline for completion, which you should employ to keep the talks going forward.

It's true that deals perish with time.

Make sure the due diligence procedure is included in the discussions.

This may necessitate reopening concerns where a significant change has occurred, but it should be done simultaneously during the negotiations and not accumulated as a long list of modifications as the deadline for closing the deal approaches.

Chapter 75: Key Learning's from the World of Conducting Negotiations and Managing Transaction Processes

Let's take a look now at the key negotiating lessons from America.

According to Getting to Yes, by Fisher and Yurie, negotiation is essentially a logical and rational process.

This book is a great introduction if you're new to negotiation.

It's also a very useful tool for learning the basics of negotiating and what your bargaining position will be.

But it's not the final word on the subject, as you'll see.

After conducting their research, they arrived at the conclusion that working with a partner and finding the best alternative to a negotiated agreement was the way to go.

So it's really your backup plan, and this is a very important notion to consider ahead of time.

You should also have a good sense of the ZOPA, or zone of possible agreement, which is essentially where you overlap with the other side and where you're willing to compromise in order to satisfy some of their conditions and demands.

In a head-to-head comparison between hard and soft negotiators, the hard negotiators usually win, even at the cost of long-term goodwill with the other party.

So, this is something to consider while comparing the other side's style to your own in order to conclude that one.

Moving on, Tversky and Curnamona Care from the Chicago School of Philosophy produced a somewhat different concept in a fantastic book, which I've read and strongly advise to you titled Thinking Fast and Slow.

They believe that the mind is made up of two parts: one, which is emotional and somewhat automatic, and two, which is logical and very straightforward but requires a lot of effort.

To make matters worse, System One is frequently incorrect and dominates system, since it's the system, one is the standard system, and system two only comes into effect if you really concentrate on stuff.

When negotiating with another party, they will most likely give you an emotional rather than a logical response.

And, of course, you have to consider how you'll communicate your ideas to get them to evaluate them rather than just feed into system one.

This may be especially true now that most companies, regardless of the industry sector, are moving to a year-round calendar. This implies that your negotiating preparation is even more crucial than ever.

One of the things you may do is conduct a SWOT analysis on both sides, including the counterparty and your own position.

Ensure that the evaluation you perform on the target is thorough.

If you're selling your company, make sure you've completed all of your valuation homework so that the other side pays the amount you want.

Check the fine print of any contract you sign—especially if there is no penalty for early withdrawal. Make sure you know where the limit is and what your walkaway position is.

If they pressure you, you'll have to back out of the transaction.

It's better to avoid making a bad agreement than to attempt it. Make sure you understand both parties' commitment to the transaction and then see if you can use this to your advantage.

If the other party is ready to make concessions, you'll be able to apply more pressure.

However, you must have a sensitivity for what will make them leave and what won't, such as whether they will buy your product or service.

But, if you have a good understanding of their commitment and what motivates them to do the transaction, you can begin to take advantage of those problems. From the start, study how they act and present information, as well as how they approach negotiations so that you may understand how they work.

Then you have options. You can respond, and you may develop your own strategies to counter or make the most of whatever tactic they're using in a negotiation.

I keep repeating this, but I say never, ever refuse anything. You might not like what they're suggesting, but consider it and come back with an alternative.

People will eventually get tired of hearing you say no and walk away if you do it enough.

So you need to find innovative methods to put your message back in a different way while retaining empathy and trust.

Make sure you take command from the start and manage the process.

You'll also need to be meticulous and up to date on all of the details, as well as making sure you're driving the process, following the schedule, maintaining momentum, and doing everything else required.

Don't sit back and let the other side take control; reciprocity is a key idea. It might be challenging to establish with some groups.

But if you can establish the notion that if you give something, you expect something in return, and you can set up this reciprocity pattern, it will be considerably simpler to conclude everything.

There's much, much more if you realize the whole of the position that the other side wants to take; this is far less likely to happen.

So, throughout a negotiation, it's always beneficial to get the other side at the start.

Then you may say, for example, "So now we've got to go back and address these items in a logical sequence."

However, don't allow them to take us off track by line negotiation until you've fully comprehended their standpoint.

Finally, once you've finished your due diligence, make sure any concerns that arise from it get immediately input into the negotiation so that they can be brought up as soon as possible and incorporated into the discussion.

The following are the main learning's from the negotiation session.

I also hope that, after reading this book, you will be more successful in your negotiations as a result of better understanding.

Chapter 76: Schedule of Events - Activity

Now we come to activity for, and I'd want to discuss a thorough timetable now during this stage of your transaction, if you don't have a detailed timetable, I'm really concerned.

A timetable is not the same thing as a calendar item. It's a really thorough paper that covers everything you'll need in your transaction, from start to finish, with each activity, event, and detail noted in chronological order.

A detailed timetable is required for every transaction. This is generally handled by buyers' advisers, and it has everything needed.

Now, I make no secret of the fact that if you don't have a timetable, your deal will not succeed.

With the end of each month fast approaching, you'll be scrambling to complete all of your tasks by then. It's just an inevitability that everything will come apart quickly after that.

Of course, every agreement is different, so I can't make your timetable for you.

An example has been given to demonstrate the principle, but you should probably start with a blank piece of paper and a calendar and add things as you go.

Consider all of the various advisers and all of the other duties that will be completed, and then put them in your calendar.

If you're not sure who's doing what, go back to those advisors and request that they set a timetable for their own activities. You may then organize everything based on their input.

Now, the most important columns are date and day, and you won't accidentally include weekend activity or comments.

You may also add parties to make it clear which persons are associated with each occasion.

This is especially crucial if you're dealing with a long-term contract. Also, make sure to include everyone's vacation dates in there since they'll be away if they're one of the key individuals.

Stop what you're doing and double-check that your timetable is complete and up to date.

Now, it goes without saying that this should be sent to all parties: buyer and seller, as well as updated on a regular basis if any substantial changes occur.

It's also worth saving the file and putting it at the top of your document so you can easily refer back to it in case there are updates.

So there's no question that someone is viewing a timetable, and it's abundantly clear that they're looking at one that is ancient and out of date. They're not aware with the most up-to-date version.

So that's your activity for this section of the book: keep this meticulous timetable correct, for heaven's sake. You will be in serious difficulties if you don't have it.

Section 13: The Sale and Purchase Agreement

Chapter 77: Sale and Purchase Agreement

The sale and purchase agreement is defined not just by your LOI, which is its origin, but also by the quality of the due diligence procedure.

This document establishes the connection between the two parties not just after closing, but also during the period before signing and closing, if problems arise.

If the issue cannot be settled, litigation is usually the next step.

The trend toward less onerous representations and warranties is eroding the significance of the S&P.

If your indemnity is limited to less than 10% of the contract value, you'll want to think long and hard before making use of it.

Another approach to reduce the hazards is to get rep and warranty insurance, which may cover misrepresentation, inaccuracy, failure to disclose, or a breach.

Private equity sellers, who are often hesitant to give long-term or high-level representations and warranties because they wish to distribute the proceeds from the sale among their partners and general partners, may now benefit from this.

Chapter 78: Concurrent Drafting

It is not always feasible to complete the due diligence before starting documentation, but short timeframes make this impossible.

Increasingly, the S&P's first draft is created straight from the LOI, with a call for greater detail as to why.

In the event that you hire a professional drafting service, there is the potential for them to take resources away from your legal firm.

It may be a challenging balancing act. We've always maintained that he or she who holds the pen has power over him.

We were talking about our preference for producing the first draft of the S&P.

The buyer generally performs this. The first draft frequently encapsulates one side's opposition, which the opposing party must spend time refuting.

At a high level, this is true. However, the more information you can provide in an LOI to prevent this, if you are the seller, the better.

Chapter 79: What are the Most Important Topics to Address During Negotiation?

The goal of the sale and purchase agreement is to clearly document the terms of the transaction between parties, allocate risks in the deal, encourage sellers to disclose as much information as possible, and provide for both parties' if anything goes wrong.

The devil is in the details.

Price inconsideration.

When it comes to pricing, things can rapidly get complicated; cash or stock, when does the money have to be paid back? The timing of payments, any postponed or contingent elements, and the impact of any working capital adjustments must all be considered during the sales and purchase agreement finalization.

In many situations, retention is a component of the consideration that is kept by the purchasers in case of possible breaches of representations and warranties, working capital changes, or contingent events like contract negotiation outcomes or existing litigation.

During bargaining, the numbers and durations of these retention's may be disputed.

In the event that after signing some parts of the seller's information, findings are found to be false or challenged, these warranties and representations are included in the S&P to provide buyer confidence in the due diligence results.

The representations and warranties are there to prove what was said in the disclosures.

Qualifiers and thresholds are often used to limit the scope of what is covered.

There is usually a timetable of facts that have been made public and to which the representations and warranties do not apply unless the information was incorrect.

Financial statements, intellectual property, contracts and liabilities are all covered by representations and warranties.

The buyer will typically guarantee that he has the legal authority to negotiate and conclude the transaction, that they have the financial wherewithal to complete it, that there are no legal issues that might jeopardize the transaction, and that they are solely responsible for any finder's fees as stated by them.

Negative and positive covenants between signing and closing, such as operating the business in the normal way, are typically focused on limiting these to what is reasonable and with appropriate time constraints.

Buyers are also required to give covenants that specify what they will do before and after the acquisition is complete.

These are a few of the many issues that HR professionals deal with on a daily basis. They might take up a significant amount of time, including compensation, benefits, and options problems.

Conditions to closing certain operations and provisions regarding compliance and consents are established for both the buyer and seller, and they must be discussed and agreed before the transaction may proceed. There may be times when one or both sides need to take action before the transaction can complete.

In the event of a breach of one or more of the representations, warranties, or covenants, the buyer will expect the seller to give an indemnity.

The final negotiations are essential, and the seller's attorneys will spend a lot of time attempting to minimize these as much as possible.

Allocation of risk.

Qualifiers are used to transfer risk from the seller's side to the buyer's.

In other words, the buyer may only enforce the condition if the seller was aware of the problem or if the scope of the issue is greater than agreed levels of materiality.

The end date of the contract is often determined by an expiration clause, which determines both parties' termination rights. If mutually agreed, the agreement may be terminated at any time.

It's always a good idea to have a process in place for resolving any disputes that may arise, including binding independent arbitration.

It's always better to avoid expensive litigation by resolving a disagreement through mediation, which is more peaceful and less stressful. In some circumstances, this may even lead to the dispute being settled without the need for court action.

Chapter 80: Complexities and Issues That May Arise

As the twin tracks of due diligence and documentation advance, be prepared for any unforeseen problems.

You may need to engage outside parties for this, since thorough research may uncover these and have a significant influence on the agreement's drafting.

Don't overlook cultural or transnational issues.

Internal cultures of organizations can vary considerably, which might lead to difficulties.

When it comes to making business agreements, don't overlook the role of global cultural distinctions.

This is a book in its own right, but don't take a typical language as the basis for cultural compatibility. In at least France and Italy, there are vast differences between northern Europeans and southern Europeans in business cultural terms.

If the buyer is simultaneously pursuing external private investors and capital market financing for the purchase, it might be more difficult to get a deal financed.

These debates may have an impact on the S&P's specific terms, especially in the later phases of a deal when issues emerge.

Remember that discussions should be devoid of emotions.

Look back to the spirit of the bargain you made at the start and search for a realistic, no-nonsense answer to the problem that won't harm your trust in each other in these tense circumstances.

In military parlance, keep your eyes on the target.

Chapter 81: Market Analyzer - Deal Review and Deal Breakers Checklist

Welcome to Activity 3. I'll need you to do a deal evaluation and go through my Deal Breakers Checklist in order to see where you stand.

Having reached the sale and purchase agreement, I now urge you to sit down with your lawyers and go through this agreement in detail, after which consider and go through the deal breakers checklist that I supplied.

It's critical that you work closely with your legal representatives on this since they'll be in command of the minute details as well as obscure language to assist you understand exactly what's in the document.

Okay, now that you've seen the checklist I supplied you with this letter, please accept that it is not comprehensive and is only for educational purposes.

So it must precisely reflect the letter of intent's specifics and the key elements of the agreement you've already hammered out.

However, go through it sentence by sentence. Consult with your lawyers about it; seek to understand what the phrases mean; and determine whether any difficulties exist that need additional discussion with the opposing side.

One of the most essential things to check is that the purchase price is correct.

Make sure you understand the purchase price completely before making a sale. Take a particularly close look at what conditions are attached to the payment of the purchase price in order to ensure that you're receiving exactly what you anticipated and that there aren't any hidden costs.

Also, if you're on the other side, make sure the company's description is correct and that you're receiving what you paid for. Check to see whether everything has been delivered as promised in all of your warranties. I'm sure you'll have a lot to talk about there.

Look at them in terms of reasonableness, as well, because one thing you can do from the seller's perspective is to negotiate when the various incentives kick in.

You can pass more of the risk on to the buyer in order for you to be certain that they were informed.

They were well aware of the situation. They took all necessary measures, among other things.

What's more, this is a fantastic technique to negotiate and reduce some of the danger in the contract.

Take a look at the working capital statements to see how the agreement expects the working capital changes to be made.

Games, for example, can be played by both the buyer and seller. Changes in operational cash flow might have a significant impact on value, and games may be devised to suit any situation.

Negotiations over working capital are frequently heated, so keep an eye on that one and then go through my succinct deal breaker checklist.

The goal of this is to get you thinking about the major concerns and to attempt to identify what will be completely unacceptable.

Maybe you can add a lot more detail to this checklist, but since every transaction is unique, I'm trying to get you in the zone and then hopefully you'll spot the specifics and come up with your own ideas as you go through the checklist to identify any deal breakers in this agreement.

The third activity for this section is to conduct the deal review and then go through my deal breakers checklist.

Section 14: Getting Your Business Ready for a Merger or Acquisition - Closing The Deal

You can't teach experience, but it's certainly not optional. This book is based on study and aims to offer some ideas that will assist you in becoming a more effective president, advisor, or negotiator.

Introduction.

After signing a letter of intent, you must now complete the next 10 to 12 weeks by navigating your deal through the due diligence and documentation phases to closing.

This isn't as simple as it sounds. The first thing to keep in mind is that the letter of intent or MOU is just a starting point for the agreement; and there's a lot of fine print still left unwritten.

Recognize that there's still a lot more that may be moved, including the price.

Remember, the LOI is a non-binding agreement. The confidentiality and exclusivity provisions are the only things that are binding.

It's not the only offer on the table. The first thing I'd want you to remember in this stage of the deal is that you are negotiating with a counterparty who isn't the only option.

The best method to ensure your business is functioning at peak efficiency is to implement the do nothing option. The do nothing option should always be an alternative if you don't have to perform a transaction.

You will get a better bargain. If you don't believe that you have any other alternatives, be ready to consider one of your alternative counterparts as soon as the LOI period of exclusivity has ended, of course. Alternatively, walk away.

Chapter 82: It's Not Only About the Money

The economics of your agreement go far beyond the headline price you need to keep in mind all of the other variables, kinds of consideration, deal structure, management, incentives, details, terms and conditions, representations and warranties, working capital, capital structure, speed, certainty and trust.

You should strive to identify the areas that are most essential to you as soon as feasible, but keep any issues on your side open.

Maintain the momentum of your situation by working at a consistent pace, but do not destroy trust through backtracking on something that has previously been agreed.

Anglo-Saxon negotiators, on the other hand, are more linear in their approach. In return for concessions on other issues, Anglo-Saxon negotiators tend to be linear and trade off issues.

Different types of negotiation are more game-like and less trading-based than other styles.

Keep an eye on the other side reopening an issue that you thought was resolved and for which you've already made a concession, in order to seek further compromises and concessions from you.

Understanding your opponent's style is an essential element of the negotiation, and some may take a strong position on certain issues, but once they've made their case, they can be persuaded to compromise and come closer to you.

Others, on the other hand, focus on less particular details and make a moral argument.

This leaves a lot more detail to work out, and it's comparable to catching eels. Just when you think you've got another one, he slips away from your grasp on the other side and raises the issue once again.

While keeping your perspective on the other side's strategy and approach, take a detached view of the game and protect your demands.

Chapter 83: Actions are more powerful than words.

Don't just pay attention to what the other side has to say, keep an eye on how they act and body language, any negotiation is a process of developing trust.

It's less significant what you say than what the opposing side does when it comes to keeping their promises.

On your side, keep track of the circumstances in which you conduct activities such as setting up meetings and how you write papers.

You might not always want to create a warm and amiable atmosphere.

In order to convey force or irritation without actually saying so, consider how and when you arrange meetings, the agenda that you create, and who and how many people are on your side.

Above all, ensure that your team is informed ahead of time so they may anticipate your game, prepare, and objectives for the meeting.

Chapter 84: Everything is Negotiable (Even When You've Signed)

While you're in the middle of a project and have a letter of intent to guide you, everything is on the table, so you'll need to be adaptable enough to react.

While the lawyers duke it out over minute details in the sale and purchase agreement, they are being directed by the principals on either side, both of whom will be seeking to gain an advantage over one another at all times.

Finally, keep in mind that each transaction is unique and has a distinct group of participants.

It's similar to going to see a Shakespeare play, but they're all unique in their own way.

Sensitivity to the personalities and egos on both sides, as well as an ability to manage the process, is critical in achieving success. You will never reach the winning line if you attempt to run a fix game plan or play a winning game of strategy.

Section 15: Closing The Deal

Chapter 85: Overcoming Obstacles While Closing an M&A Deal

A deal is made up of three parts: the amount of money you will receive when you acquire it, and why you may have to return it.

You must realize that this segment of the discussion will be competitive and adversarial, your greatest obstacle on either side is to continuously build and develop a trusting relationship.

As the agreement moves on, there is no replacing moderation in eating and drinking at certain intervals throughout the deal.

Make these events social, and avoid talking about business at all, especially if you're attempting to overcome something difficult.

At dinner on the day following, you'll be much more constructive and objective on both sides. That is, in fact, my experience.

If you're having difficulties addressing key issues, it's tempting to just seek indemnity so you can move on.

There might be issues agreeing on the amounts in terms of earn-out payments or the influence of future contingent events after closing. It's critical to ensure that your operation is running smoothly at this point.

Check for errors in the draft. Any expert opinions or reports should be provided in a timely manner and appropriately considered before being incorporated into the drafting.

You must be prepared, or you will make mistakes. Consider how the latest financial data would be updated, for example, and whether a short deed and paperwork period reduces the risk that these values may change after they have been agreed upon on the basis of a set of financial forecasts.

They can, however, in the event of a significant unforeseen catastrophe affecting the company's success.

This may be either a good or bad thing, depending on how you look at it. I've been in a position to bargain over the acquisition of a fast-growing firm, which constantly tried to change the terms as the company grew.

We never seem to get a handle on it. Commercial confidentiality agreements, which the seller will be hesitant to reveal too early in the process, might cause unexpected difficulties.

These are frequently difficult because the parties to the contract are rivals, and the information in them is commercially sensitive and possibly harmful if leaked. And the deal does not close.

Be on the lookout for change of control provisions in commercial contracts with clients and suppliers, too.

Losing a substantial proportion of either type of customer after a deal has closed might have a severely negative influence on the business immediately after the closing.

When everyone is attempting to focus on post-deal implementation, which may include significant management adjustments, it's easy for something else to slip through the cracks.

It's critical to conduct a thorough examination of all licensing agreements and intellectual property to ensure there are no unforeseen issues.

When the seller is attempting to manage the procedure so that documentation of the agreement doesn't go too far ahead of at least preliminary due diligence findings, they should always be trying to ensure that any material information is passed on early, even if some very sensitive data is withheld for a few weeks.

It's more likely that the buyer will attempt renegotiation if material knowledge emerges at a later date.

The seller's negotiating position deteriorates as the duration of the agreement increases.

Chapter 86: Keep the Principals Involved

Once you begin the post-LOI procedure, you'll want a clear schedule for deal signing and closure.

In order to do so, it's critical to keep the principles of the agreement engaged in order to allow informed and timely decisions.

When the negotiators return to head office, any process that is continuously put on hold while they check in is likely to encounter difficulties.

This implies that both people and the exchange must be held accountable for the S&P's content on both sides.

It's critical that you have a strong engage team of consultants on both sides, and their transaction experience can help to move things along if they're familiar with similar problems and know how to negotiate and document.

It also helps if your advisors are familiar with negotiating terms and negotiating methods that they may have seen during previous negotiations with the counterparty.

Chapter 87: Closing Deal Points

Closing deal points is one of the most important phases in obtaining a contract over the finish line. Agreeing early on that any bargain point that has been agreed cannot be reopened is a crucial step.

When dealing with southerly European or Asian counterparts, you may struggle to attain this.

It's a question of culture and lifestyle. If you don't do this, the discussions and negotiations will eventually come full circle, starting again.

At the end of the day, you must be prepared to call it a day.

It's possible that there are some non-negotiable concerns on the other side of the table that you can't reach an agreement on.

While we all want to be tenacious and loathe to see a bargain fail, in the end, a terrible agreement is unlikely to get closed or there will be substantial difficulties between the parties after closure.

Chapter 88: Deal Closing - Timing

On rare occasions, when shareholder agreement or regulatory permissions are required, we all want to accomplish a simultaneous signing and closing. This is not feasible.

Closing a business always entails extra danger of poor performance during the time between signing and closing.

This might also result in lengthy discussions about who should absorb the risk during this time.

A simultaneous closing eliminates risk, complexity, and cost while also providing security for both parties after a contract is signed.

A disadvantage of not having a formalized selling management structure is that there is a danger the leadership and employees will disconnect, resulting in reduced company performance.

If the transaction does not go through, the company is harmed and the management must begin again with more issues than they had when they began.

Chapter 89: Closing - Complexities

Closing a transaction is more than simply obtaining a signature on a legally binding instrument; there are often a number of events that must occur simultaneously as soon as possible, not the least of which is the wire transfer of money.

Lawyers must figure out how to hold a closing meeting in the cramped confines of an office, where people spend much of their day hunched over their computers. Typically, this entails getting all parties to their offices, usually until 3:00 a.m., when a huge table strains under heaps of papers, contracts, and documents for approval.

These can include board and shareholder issues, corporate resolutions and authorizations, legal opinions, additional supporting materials including employment and escrow agreements, the consideration cash or shares, financing agreements, regulatory approvals, and evidence of third-party concerns such as change of control consents where necessary.

Non-competing non-solicitation agreements should be prepared and in place before signing, and they should endure after the contract is signed.

Don't overlook the intricacy if you have competent attorneys on your side; this is unlikely to be an issue if you work with a legal firm that isn't an M&A specialist, but it can cause significant headaches.

You've been forewarned.

Chapter 90: In Person or Virtual Closing?

I generally prefer to have everyone at the table sign the contract, but virtual closings are becoming more widespread.

We all have busy lives, and getting major businesses to release time for senior management to travel across countries to attend a closing may be difficult.

The terms of the agreement must be made available for the whole 24 hours before it is finalized to allow for any last-minute concerns to be addressed promptly.

Summary.

The due diligence process and the deal documentation necessitate a large amount of work and dedication from both parties to ensure that the transaction does close, and attention to detail is required to guarantee that the true value of the arrangement is recorded and realized for both sides.

The success of the process will be determined by how well it is organized, and the competence of the parties' principal and adviser teams will be evident in the efficiency of the process and probability of its ultimate success even after closing.

Chapter 91: Activity: Deal Closing Checklist

The deal is the final activity for the book. Every deal is, of course, unique, so I can't create your checklist for you.

Here's a sample outline for you to use. I want to make it clear that this is only for academic reasons.

Make sure you work with your attorneys to develop this checklist so that you're certain you have it all itemized, and that you understand what needs to be done and what documentation you'll need at closing.

To begin, you'll establish a list of all the attendees who will be responsible for recording and taking actions at the meeting.

So it's worth creating a sort of list at the top, with those items organized into groups. So you can identify them immediately.

Then, to assign them tasks in the checklist's detail, you match them to their initials.

You'll need a variety of columns for this sort of thing. Yes, it's in writing, although it may be called anything else you want.

The party who will actually put the document in motion (deliver it), establish the document's status, and sign and clear off any issues with it only then is known.

Definitely collaborate with both sets of attorneys on this. They will be able to put together this timetable with you, but you must comprehend what's required and keep an eye out for any omissions that would require the closing meeting to miss or have to be postpone due to a missing crucial document.

The documentation is divided into four categories.

You'll have your initial paperwork, such as a sale and purchase agreement, any pre-closing documentation that must be completed before you can finish the closing documents, and then any post-closing actions, such as a name change or other adjustments.

These are the primary headings, but you'll find further information in the template.

I've also included a checklist for you to use in creating your own list, although I advise you to trust your lawyers and attorneys to obtain the specifics of this.

That's all there is to it for this section: your ideal closing checklist. So get started and double-check that you've not overlooked anything important.

Section 16: Summary and Wrap Up

Chapter 92 - Summary and Wrap Up

I hope you've completed this book and that, while there's a lot of complexity in it, because I've attempted to cover this theme in a series of overlapping chapters, you're beginning to see how the whole thing hangs together.

Because everything impacts on everything else, it's difficult to establish truly distinctive and entirely stand-alone sections.

I began by walking you through the topic, going through all of the steps involved in a merger or acquisition, and then took you on a fun section that was all about the M&A game. It provided you with an easy and lighthearted introduction to it before hitting you with the valuation crash course, which is really quite difficult business school-style learning.

Following, we went through several parts of the whole selling a business procedure.

We took a look at the beginning stages and presale preparation.

We investigated how to go about the sale process.

We also spoke about marketing the company before moving on to a part where we reviewed some of the most essential topics in a corporate sale, but particularly from the perspective of a buyout.

I then walked you through some term sheet issues and gave you a basic introduction to the procedure and negotiation skills.

Then we get to where we are now and finish up, just to state that this book will develop into an organic league-wide growth text.

Remember, I'm here to assist you. I'm really enthusiastic about getting to know you better.

If you have any questions, especially those regarding topics I haven't addressed, please do not hesitate to contact me since it would motivate me to include them in the book.

All you have to do now is send me a direct message through the Discord group. It's really simple.

Consider leaving a review if you found value in this book.

If you're unhappy with the book, I'd rather hear from you before rating and reviewing it so that we can figure out how to resolve the concerns you're dissatisfied with.

I'd also like to discover more about your professional background and acquire some pointers from you regarding the concerns you want addressed. We'll have a lot more to offer in the book if you work with me on this and it will be a lot better for everyone as a result of increased content.

That concludes our discussion of corporate finance. I'm hoping you found it beneficial, interesting, enthralling, and that it will aid you in your business endeavors.

Chapter 93: Bonus Resources You Wouldn't Want to Miss

I recommend that you listen to my **60-Day Startup Launch Blueprint Podcast**. It's a new Podcast that I'm working on. And there you'll discover many episodes regarding a business model and innovation.

You could also checkout my '**60 Day Start-up Launch Blueprint**' Course to Discover, Validate and Launch your Start-up Ideas Profitably under 60 Days: https://www.udemy.com/course/60-day-startup

As a parting gift I want to give you my **40 – Million Dollar Startup Ideas**, which you can implement in the now and start making bank.

Shut-Up! And Steal My Ideas – Volume 1

https://www.amazon.com/dp/B0979TWV44

Shut-Up! And Steal My Ideas – Volume 2

https://www.amazon.com/dp/B0999SQMCY

You can choose to stay in touch via Social handles of your choice.

Looking forward to your feedback on this book on either of the Social media handles or if you prefer to write to me directly, here's my email again: umran@onecallbusinesssolutions.com

P.S I answer all my emails myself. _Feel comfortable sharing brutal troll worthy feedback._ Everything goes. **No Filters**! Cheers!

Umran Nayani

Printed in Great Britain
by Amazon